# PREFACE

Since the first printing of ARLINGTON HERIT-AGE,* there has been much continued interest in the publication of a companion book on the adjacent area. To meet this historical and educational need, NORTH-ERN VIRGINIA HERITAGE is offered as a pictorial history of the upper portion of the "Northern Neck" of Virginia. Possibly no other state has had more books written on its beautiful homes and historical sites, but, except for mention of the museum houses, this area has been virtually ignored. North of the Rappahannock River and on up the Potomac is a land rich in history and beauty.

The first compilation of historic sites and homes in the area totalled six hundred and fifty, which was reduced to four hundred and forty-four. The format of the book necessitated the omission of many interesting homes. The selection shows a cross-section of various types symbolizing different aspects of pioneer, Colonial and Early Federal life; from cabins to mansions, constructed of log, clapboard, brick, and stone. Included are pictures of several old homes which are now gone, victims of the elements or the bull-dozers. Some outstanding examples of Twentieth Century structures are included which will endure as beautiful examples of current architecture. Tucked in are a few places where one can dine in an atmosphere of Virginia tradition and hospitality. In the case of homes, we have endeavored to protect the privacy of the current owners by not mentioning their names.

No attempt has been made to give a detailed history of each county or area, but, instead, the over-all beauty, heritage, and mellow charm of the portion of Virginia which has never before been comprehensively covered in a pictorial book. The book does contain a brief history of the entire area and of each county, with copious captions for individual pictures. The narration follows the flow of settlement up the Potomac from the narrow strip of land between it and the Rappahannock at Fredericksburg, to its confluence with the Shenandoah at Harpers Ferry. From there to the headwaters of the Rappahannock, the boundary of the area follows the crest of the Blue Ridge, along which winds the Appalachian Trail. The areas then described sweep over the Piedmont Plateau fan-wise from the Potomac southward.

The fascinating past linked to the interesting present is important to the continuity of the history of Virginia. We have brought together the combined efforts of many historians, in addition to a great deal of original research and discovery. As word of the project spread, we received heart-warming encouragement and cooperation from historians, historical societies, chambers of commerce, and the general public. We believe that NORTHERN VIRGINIA HERITAGE will stimulate the interest of readers to delve further into the history of this portion of the Old Dominion. A bibliography of books which we found very informative has been provided.

It is believed that this volume will be of national interest, for this is the land of our early statesmen, the founders of America. It may surprise residents of many distant states to learn that their areas were once considered part of the "Kingdom of Virginia". Many of the nationally famous shrines, museum houses, and attractions associated with Washington are really part of our NORTHERN VIRGINIA HERITAGE.

ELEANOR LEE TEMPLEMAN
NAN NETHERTON

* ARLINGTON HERITAGE, Vignettes of a Virginia County.

This book, first published in 1959, is currently in its sixth printing. It is handsomely bound, profusely illustrated companion book to NORTHERN VIRGINIA HERITAGE. A detailed study of Arlington County, the Virginia portion of the original District of Columbia until 1846, it includes the human interest stories of the pioneer families.

Available through ELEANOR LEE TEMPLEMAN, 3001 North Pollard Street, Arlington, Virginia 22207. Price $6.50, plus 50¢ mailing expense.

We dedicate this book

with deep appreciation

to all those who have encouraged

and assisted us in its compilation

and to those who

during the past three and a half centuries,

by their valor have created

the heritage which we cherish.

WASHINGTON RETURNING FROM THE HUNT
By John Ward Dunsmore. Original at Fraunces Tavern,
New York Historical Society.

© Eleanor Lee Templeman 1966

Library of Congress catalog card number 66-29716

First Edition, December 1966

Second Printing, November 1967

Third Printing, January 1971 (Revised)

Available through

ELEANOR LEE TEMPLEMAN
3001 North Pollard Street
Arlington, Virginia 22207

# Northern Virginia Heritage

A PICTORIAL COMPILATION

OF THE HISTORIC SITES AND HOMES

in the counties of

ARLINGTON, FAIRFAX, LOUDOUN,

FAUQUIER, PRINCE WILLIAM and STAFFORD,

and the cities of

ALEXANDRIA and FREDERICKSBURG

by

ELEANOR LEE TEMPLEMAN

and

NAN NETHERTON

Privately published

by

Eleanor Lee Templeman

1966

# TABLE OF CONTENTS

# THE INCONVENIENCIES

## THAT HAVE HAPPENED TO SOME PER-
## SONS WHICH HAVE TRANSPORTED THEMSELVES

from *England* to *Virginia*, vvithout prouisions neceſſary to ſuſtaine themſelues, hath
*greatly hindred the Progreſſe of that noble Plantation: For preuention of the like diſorders*
heereafter, that no man ſuffer, either through ignorance or miſinformation; it is thought re-
quiſite to publiſh this ſhort declaration: wherein is contained a particular of ſuch neceſ-
*ſaries, as either priuate families or ſingle perſons ſhall haue cauſe to furniſh themſelues with, for their better*
*ſupport at their firſt landing in* Virginia; *whereby alſo greater numbers may receiue in part,*
*directions how to prouide themſelues.*

### Apparrell.

| | | li. | s. | d. |
|---|---|---|---|---|
| One Monmouth Cap | | ∞ | 01 | 10 |
| Three falling bands | | — | 01 | 03 |
| Three ſhirts | | — | 07 | c6 |
| One waſte-coate | | — | 02 | 02 |
| One ſuite of Canuaſe | | — | 07 | 06 |
| One ſuite of Frize | | — | 10 | 00 |
| One ſuite of Cloth | | — | 15 | 00 |
| Three paire of Iriſh ſtockins | | — | 04 | 00 |
| Foure paire of ſhooes | | — | c8 | c8 |
| One paire of garters | | — | 00 | 10 |
| One doozen of points | | — | 00 | 03 |
| One paire of Canuaſe ſheets | | — | c8 | 00 |
| Seuen ells of Canuaſe, to make a bed and boulſter, to be filled in *Virginia* 8.s. | | | | |
| One Rug for a bed 8. s. which with the bed ſeruing for two men, halfe is | | — | c8 | 00 |
| Fiue ells coorſe Canuaſe, to make a bed at Sea for two men, to be filled with ſtraw, iiij. s. | | | | |
| One coorſe Rug at Sea for two men, will coſt vj. s. is for one | | — | 05 | 00 |
| | | 04 | 00 | 00 |

*Apparrell for one man, and ſo after the rate for more.*

### Victuall.

| | | li. | s. | d. |
|---|---|---|---|---|
| Eight buſhels of Meale | | 02 | 00 | 00 |
| Two buſhels of peaſe at 3.s. | | — | 06 | 00 |
| Two buſhels of Oatemeale 4.s. 6.d. | | — | 09 | 00 |
| One gallon of *Aquauitæ* | | — | 02 | 06 |
| One gallon of Oyle | | — | 03 | 06 |
| Two gallons of Vineger 1. s. | | — | 02 | 00 |
| | | 03 | 03 | 00 |

*For a whole yeere for one man, and ſo for more after the rate.*

### Armes.

| | | li. | s. | d. |
|---|---|---|---|---|
| One Armour compleat, light | | — | 17 | 00 |
| One long Peece, fiue foot or fiue and a halfe, neere Musket bore | | 01 | 02 | 00 |
| One ſword | | — | 05 | — |
| One belt | | — | 01 | — |
| One bandaleere | | — | 01 | 06 |
| Twenty pound of powder | | — | 18 | 00 |
| Sixty pound of ſhot or lead, Piſtoll and Gooſe ſhot | | — | 05 | 00 |
| | | 03 | 09 | 06 |

*For one man, but if halfe of your men haue armour it is ſufficient ſo that all haue Peeces and ſwords.*

### Tooles.

| | | li. | s. | d. |
|---|---|---|---|---|
| Fiue broad howes at 2.s. a piece | | — | 10 | — |
| Fiue narrow howes at 16.d. a piece | | — | 06 | c8 |
| Two broad Axes at 3.5. 8.d. a piece | | — | 07 | c4 |
| Fiue felling Axes at 18.d. a piece | | — | 07 | 06 |
| Two ſteele hand ſawes at 16.d. a piece | | — | 02 | 08 |
| Two two-hand-ſawes at 5. s. a piece | | — | 10 | — |
| One whip-ſaw, ſet and filed with box, file, and wreſt | | — | 10 | — |
| Two hammers 12.d. a piece | | — | 02 | 00 |
| Three ſhouels 18.d. a piece | | — | 04 | 06 |
| Two ſpades at 18.d. a piece | | — | 03 | — |
| Two augers 6.d. a piece | | — | 01 | 00 |
| Six chiſſels 6.d. a piece | | — | 03 | 00 |
| Two percers ſtocked 4.d. a piece | | — | 00 | c8 |
| Three gimlets 2.d. a piece | | — | 00 | c6 |
| Two hatchets 21.d. a piece | | — | 03 | 06 |
| Two froues to cleaue pale 18.d. | | — | 03 | 00 |
| Two hand-bills 20. a piece | | — | 03 | 04 |
| One grindleſtone 4.s. | | — | 04 | 00 |
| Nailes of all ſorts to the value of | | 02 | 00 | — |
| Two Pickaxes | | — | c3 | — |
| | | c6 | c2 | c8 |

*For a family of 6. perſons and ſo after the rate for more.*

### Houſhold Implements.

| | | li. | s. | d. |
|---|---|---|---|---|
| One Iron Pot | | co | 07 | — |
| One kettle | | — | 06 | — |
| One large frying-pan | | — | 02 | c6 |
| One gridiron | | — | 01 | 06 |
| Two ſkillets | | — | 05 | — |
| One ſpit | | — | 02 | — |
| Platters, diſhes, ſpoones of wood | | — | 04 | — |
| | | c1 | c8 | 00 |

*For a family of 6. perſons, and ſo for more or leſſe after the rate.*

| | | li. | s. | d. |
|---|---|---|---|---|
| For Suger, Spice, and fruit, and at Sea for 6 men | | ∞ | 12 | c6 |
| So the full charge of Apparrell, Victuall, Armes, Tooles, and houſhold ſtuffe, and after this rate for each perſon, will amount vnto about the ſumme of | | 12 | 10 | — |
| The paſſage of each man is | | 06 | 00 | — |
| The fraight of theſe prouiſions for a man, will bee about halfe a Tun, which is | | 01 | 10 | — |
| So the whole charge will amount to about | | 20 | 00 | 00 |

*Nets, hookes, lines, and a tent muſt be added, if the number of people be grea-*
*ter, as alſo ſome kine.*
*And thus is the vſuall proportion that the* Virginia Company *doe*
*beſtow vpon their Tenants which they ſend.*

Whoſoeuer tranſports himſelfe or any other at his owne charge vnto *Virginia*, ſhall for each perſon ſo tranſported before Midſummer 1625.
haue to him and his heires for euer fifty Acres of Land vpon a firſt, and fifty Acres vpon a ſecond diuiſion.

Imprinted at London by FELIX KYNGSTON. 1622.

# The Northern Neck Proprietary

IN 1632 King Charles I saw fit to grant to Cecil Calvert, Baron of Baltimore, all that part of Virginia lying north of the south shore of the Potomac. In effect, the King delegated to the Proprietor, Lord Baltimore, the prerogatives of the Crown with respect to the government of that area and the granting of lands there.

In 1649 King Charles II, then a refugee in France, granted to six loyal followers all the land between the Potomac and Rappahannock rivers up to the falls. That was the only way in which he could compensate them for their services. This grant was not a mere scrap of paper. Charles was then the acknowledged king in Scotland, Ireland, Virginia, and other dominions beyond the seas, was in command of the English navy, and was about to launch an attack to recover his throne in England. It was rendered a dead letter by Oliver Cromwell's decisive victory at Worcester in 1650.

The restoration of King Charles to his throne in 1660 revived the grant of 1649. In 1662 the King expressly ordered the Governor and Council in Virginia to put it into effect. They, however, saw it not only as a threat to all existing land titles in the Northern Neck, but also as a step toward creating another Maryland on the territory of Virginia. Their remonstrances and appeals for reconsideration had the effect of nullifying the royal grant until 1688, when a compromise settlement was reached. The terms of that settlement guaranteed the continuing jurisdiction of Virginia over the Northern Neck and the existing land titles in that area, which was extended westward from the falls to the headwaters of the Potomac and the Rappahannock. Thomas Culpeper, Baron of Thoresway, who had bought out the other interests in the grant of 1649, would receive the quitrents which the existing landholders had hitherto paid to the Crown, and all the unappropriated lands remaining in the area would be his to grant on similar terms.

Lord Culpeper died in 1689 and the proprietorship of the Northern Neck then passed to his only child, Lady Catherine Fairfax. At her death in 1719 it passed to her son Thomas Fairfax, sixth Baron Fairfax of Cameron, then a student at Oxford.

Settlement beyond the falls of the Potomac and the Rappahannock was hindered by the hostility of the Indians: first the Susquehannocks, who had been driven from Pennsylvania by the Iroquois, and then the Iroquois themselves. That obstacle was removed in 1722, when the Iroquois ceded to Virginia their lands south of the Potomac and east of the Blue Ridge. In 1744 they similarly ceded their lands west of the mountains.

Although the Fairfax proprietorship made no change in the government of the Northern Neck, it did make a significant change in the system of granting land. In Virginia land had hitherto been granted only on the basis of headrights (50 acres for each person brought into the colony), and grants had been subject to forfeiture if not developed within three years. These provisions were designed to promote the peopling and development of the country. The Proprietor, however, was interested only in collecting quitrents. If willing to pay the quitrents, wealthy men such as Robert Carter of Corotoman and Thomas Lee of Stratford could engross vast acreages of Fairfax land and hold them undeveloped. Such men did acquire large estates in the newly opened area, but did not develop them as plantations. The settlers who swarmed into the western parts of the Northern Neck after 1722 were small farmers: English emigrants from Tidewater seeking better fortune on the frontier, or German and Scotch-Irish immigrants from Pennsylvania. The great landholders leased farms to them, the customary lease being for three lives— that is, for the lifetimes of the original tenant, his widow, and his heir. The heirs of the great landholders came later, generally after the Revolution, bringing the plantation system with them then, while the children of the former tenants moved on to seek their fortunes farther west.

With the progress of settlement new counties were established in the Northern Neck. The remoter parts of Stafford County became Prince William County in 1731. It included all the land between the Potomac, the Rappahanock, and the Blue Ridge, except the residual Stafford County. In 1742 that part of Prince William north of the Occoquan and Bull Run became Fairfax County. In 1757 the western part of Fairfax became Loudoun County, and two years later the southwestern and western parts of Prince William became Fauquier.

In 1747 Lord Fairfax himself came to reside in Virginia and in 1752 he established his home at "Greenway Court" on the Shenandoah. There he lived in comfort, but with a rustic simplicity which any moderately prosperous Virginia planter would have considered unsuited to his own social position.

Lord Fairfax, himself a Whig, was sympathetic to American resistance to the Tory Ministry, but not to the disruption of the British Empire. During the Revolution he remained quietly on his estate in Virginia. In 1779 the Commonwealth confiscated the estates of British subjects who by failing to take an oath of allegiance to the United States had shown themselves to be, presumably, "inimical to the liberties of America", but the old Proprietor was left undisturbed. When he died in 1781, however, leaving his estate to a nephew in England, the Commonwealth promptly expropriated the Fairfax Proprietary.

The litigation which ensued continued until 1816. In brief, the landholders in the Northern Neck ceased paying quitrents and held their lands in fee simple. The Fairfax heirs were ultimately allowed to retain the lands which Lord Fairfax had appropriated for his personal use. The lands which remained unappropriated were taken over by the Commonwealth.

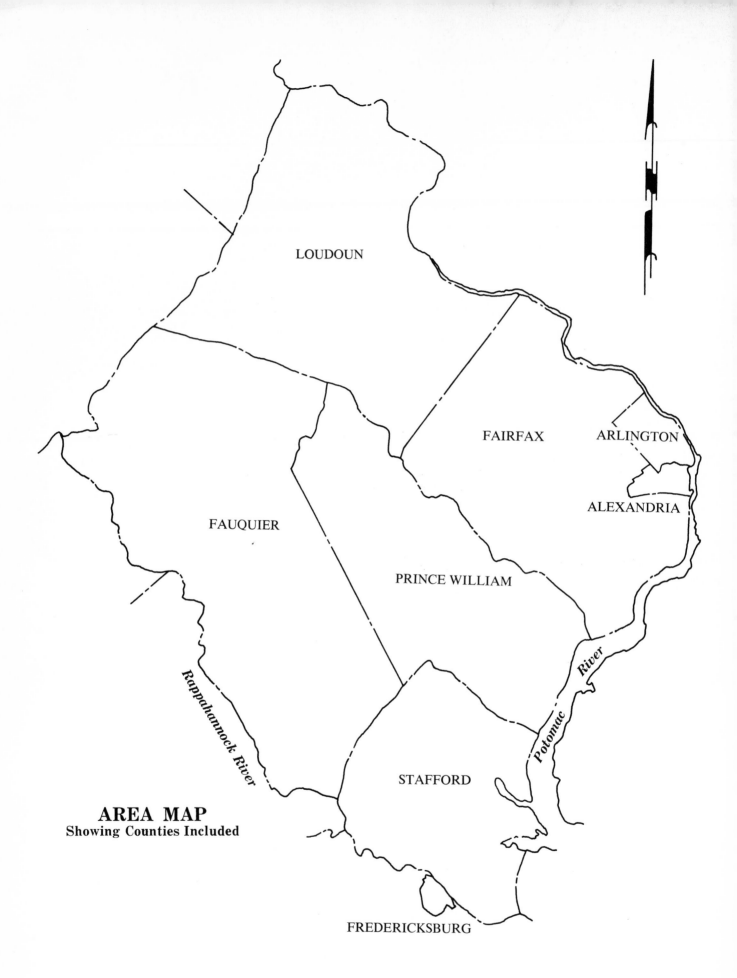

**AREA MAP**
Showing Counties Included

LOUDOUN

FAIRFAX

ARLINGTON

ALEXANDRIA

FAUQUIER

PRINCE WILLIAM

*Rappahannock River*

*Potomac River*

STAFFORD

FREDERICKSBURG

NECOSTIN INDIANS . . Exhibit of local Indian family group, using figures from the Smithsonian Institution.

# Up the Potomac in Early Times

CAPTAIN JOHN SMITH'S MAP OF VIRGINIA . . .

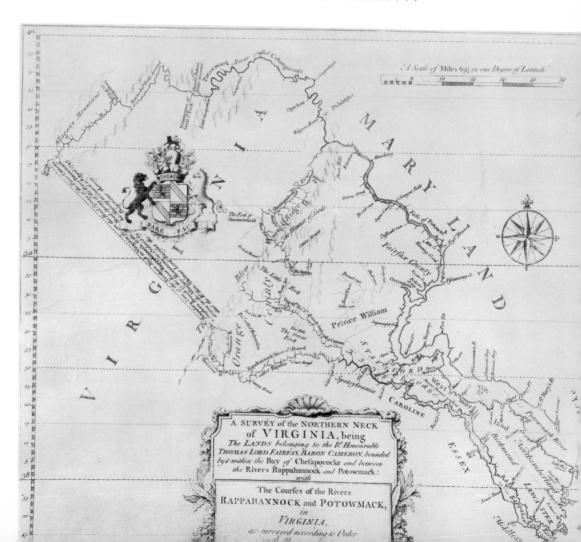

WASHINGTON'S HOUSE AT MT. VERNON

VIEW ON THE POTOMAC RIVER FROM MT. VERNON, 1798

ARLINGTON HOUSE . . . From J. W. Moore's *Picturesque Washington*

WASHINGTON FROM ARLINGTON HEIGHTS . . .

A TOURNAMENT . . . Jousting at "Analostan", the home erected about 1800 by John Mason, son of George Mason of Gunston Hall. This was on the island now known as Theodore Roosevelt Island, which has had many names including Analostan, Anacostian, Barbadoes, My Lord's Island, and Mason's Island.

CHAIN BRIDGE . . . Located at the Indian crossing just below Little Falls which Captain John Smith visited in 1608. The first wooden structure, known as the Falls Bridge, built in 1797, was replaced by another in 1804 which was destroyed by a flood. In 1808 a suspension bridge was built with chains having four and a half foot links anchored in low stone towers. Even though it has been replaced numerous times, the name "Chain Bridge" has persisted.

THE GREAT FALLS . . . to quote John Davis, 1805, "I now ascended a hill that led to the Great Falls and on a sudden my steps were suspended by the conflicts of elements, the strife of nature. I beheld the course of a large river abruptly obstructed by rocks, over which it was breaking with a tremendous roar; while the foam of the water seemed ascending to the clouds, and the shores that confined it seemed to tremble at the convolutions."

TOBACCO ROLLING ROAD . . .
Roads were cleared to enable the planters to market their tobacco crops which were packed into hogsheads and rolled down to the river wharves for shipment to England.

HARPERS FERRY, WEST VIRGINIA . . . Named for Robert Harper who settled there in 1747 to operate a ferry at the confluence of the Shenandoah and Potomac Rivers. To the right tower the Virginia Palisades, with Maryland at the upper left side. Viewed from Jefferson Rock in Harpers Ferry, one recalls that statesman's description: "The passage of the Potomac through the Blue Ridge is perhaps one of the most stupendous scenes in nature. This scene is worth a voyage across the Atlantic."

COUNTRY ROAD AND OX CART . . . Commercial competition between Alexandria and Georgetown led to the construction of toll roads, called turnpikes, financed by stock companies formed by merchants of the competing ports.

# Fredericksburg Heritage

RECORDED history of the Fredericksburg area began with the one hundred and thirty mile trip which John Smith made up the Rappahannock from Chesapeake Bay to the falls in 1608. He noted that the Mannahoak Indians lived there. The German explorer, John Lederer, mapped the vicinity in 1670 when he travelled up the Rappahannock River and recorded many facts about the natural resources of the area.

In 1671, Governor William Berkeley issued a grant later called the "Leaseland" for 2,000 acres at the Fredericksburg site to John Buckner and Thomas Royston. The Virginia House of Burgesses directed that a fort be built at or near the falls of the Rappahannock to protect the sparse settlements of pioneers to the south from Indian attacks. It was from Buckner and Royston that William Levingston leased land in the early 1700's when he and his wife Sukey came to the wilderness. As one historian put it, they came "armed with ax, musket and frying pan" and opened up a coffee house about a mile below the falls on land which became the central part of Fredericksburg when the town was chartered in 1727, named after the then Prince of Wales.

Between 1722 and 1729, Thomas Thornton secured a license to conduct an ordinary at the Ferry Landing and it was probably in existence when Fredericksburg was established. William Hunter, who owned the land, was bondsman for Thornton, who guaranteed to keep a clean, wholesome ordinary serving diets at one shilling each and not to sell anyone more drink than was necessary.

Colonel William Byrd, whose delightful writings greatly enriched the early records of the colonies, wrote in 1732, " Colonel Willis walked me about this town in Fredericksburg . . . Though this be a commodious and beautiful situation for a Town, with the advantage of a Navigable River, and Wholesome Air, yet the Inhabitants are very few. Besides Colonel Willis, who is top man of the place, there are only One Merchant, a Tailor, a Smith, and an Ordinary-keeper; though I must not forget Mrs. Levingstone, who acts here in the double capacity of a Doctress and Coffee Woman, and were this a populous city, she is qualified to exercise 2 other callings . . . It is said that the Courthouse and the Church are going to be built here, and then both religion and justice will help to enlarge the place."

Used extensively by historians and cartographers was the record of a Fredericksburg man who explored the Kentucky wilderness twenty years before the more publicized journey of Daniel Boone. Valuable geographical and topographical data were compiled in "First Explorations of Kentucky, Journals of Dr. Thomas Walker, 1750."

Fredericksburg developed into an important commercial center during the next few decades. This was due to its location on the river and also on the main road between Virginia and the Middle Colonies. Trade was carried on with more than one hundred and twenty-five other ports, the staples were grain, flour and tobacco and by the beginning of the 1800's the annual average sales were $4,000,000.

During the Revolutionary War, the town was of great strategic importance because of Fielding Lewis' Gunnery and Hunter's Iron Works. The head of the latter, James Hunter, is one of the forgotten heroes of history. He became postmaster for the southern part of the country when Benjamin Franklin was put in charge of the northern portion. He was Director of Public Works for Fredericksburg as well as the ironworks and there is much early documentation showing that he was an important figure in the successful struggle for independence. He incurred heavy debts financing arms and military equipment during the Revolution. When he died his creditors stole his body and paraded it through the streets.

Because of its strategic location, Fredericksburg changed hands seven times during the Civil War. It was devastated by heavy bombardment which preceded the bloody battle in December, 1862, resulting in casualties on both sides amounting to almost ten per cent of the 200,000 troops involved in the engagement.

The present Courthouse was built in 1852 in the Victorian style on the site which has been used for the purpose since 1732.

The Information Center is located at the north end of Fredericksburg where maps of historic places are available and there is a National Park Service Center Museum at Lafayette Boulevard and Sunken Road.

THE OLD STONE WAREHOUSE . . . Oldest building in the city, erected about 1727, on the bank of the Rappahannock River. Reputed to have been built of ballast stone from sailing vessels, it has been used both as a warehouse and a jail. Restored by Historic Fredericksburg, Incorporated.

KENMORE . . . Built in 1752 by the noted patriot Colonel Fielding Lewis whose wife was Betty Washington, sister of George Washington. It is famous for its exquisite ceilings and overmantels, and its authentic furnishings include many Lewis and Washington heirlooms. The home was restored in 1922, by the Kenmore Association; the gardens in 1929 by The Garden Club of Virginia.

THE GUNNERY SPRING . . . In 1775 the Virginia Convention voted to establish in or near Fredericksburg a "manufactory" of arms. It was built near Hazel Run at a fine spring. One of the five commissioners appointed to superintend the work was Colonel Fielding Lewis, who mortgaged his home and estate to finance the venture. Later converted to the Old Fredericksburg Academy.

MARY WASHINGTON HOUSE . . . Erected in 1761 by Michael Robinson, from whom it was purchased in 1772 and enlarged by the General for his mother who resided there until her death in 1789. Her sundial still stands in the garden surrounded by boxwood which she planted. Preserved by the Mary Washington Branch, Association for the Preservation of Virginia Antiquities.

BROMPTON . . . Central portion built about 1740, a rear addition at an unknown date. John Lawrence Marye added the front portion in 1836 at which time it became known as the "Marye House", although it is believed its present name was used by the family out of affection for their former home in Brompton, England. Italian marble mantels originally intended for the White House but rejected because of slight imperfections, were acquired by Mr. Marye. In 1947 the home became the residence of the Chancellor of Mary Washington College, the women's college of the University of Virginia.

E. LEE TRINKLE LIBRARY . . . Named in honor of a former Governor of Virginia who was President of the State Board of Education for many years.

THE AMPHITHEATRE . . . Situated on a hillside in a grove of beautiful native trees on the campus of Mary Washington College.

HUGH MERCER APOTHECARY SHOP . . .
Operated from 1761 until his death by Dr. Hugh
Mercer of Scotland, it is said to be the earliest
drug store in America.

RISING SUN TAVERN . . . Built in 1760 by Charles Washington, it became a favorite meeting place of early statesmen. Here the Virginia Society of the Cincinnati held its first banquet, October 6, 1783. Preserved by the Mary Washington Branch, Association for the Preservation of Virginia Antiquities.

JAMES MONROE LAW OFFICE
AND MEMORIAL LIBRARY . . .
Featured with Monroe possessions
used in the White House, including
Louis XVI furniture from France
and the desk on which the Monroe
Doctrine was formulated. Walled
garden contains a fine bust of
Monroe. Owned by the University
of Virginia.

FEDERAL HILL . . . Records in the Library of Congress state, "After the Revolutionary War, Governor Robert Brooke of Virginia bought a house in Fredericksburg and renamed it 'Federal Hill' after the Federalist Party of which he was a founder."

THE QUARTERS . . . Erected about 1820 as a kitchen with servants quarters above for the adjacent Dogget House.

SAINT JAMES . . . Erected in 1759 by Fielding Lewis. An indenture from him to George Washington reads, "Yielding and paying the rent of one peppercorn upon the Feastday of St. Michael, the Archangel". General Washington later sold the house to James Mercer who named it after the Mercer estate in Scotland. The basic construction is of brick noggin with clapboard exterior and a rare gambrel roof. The brick kitchen was built in 1850 to replace an earlier one destroyed by fire; now connected to the main house by an addition built in 1963.

THE MAURY HOUSE . . . First owned by Roger Dixon about 1750, it later became the home of the great geographer, Matthew Fontaine Maury (1806-1873), called the "Pathfinder of the Seas". He was a Naval officer, scientist and the author of standard texts on navigation. In 1841 he was appointed to the Navy Department's Depot of Charts and Instruments through which he developed the Naval Observatory and the Hydrographic Office.

SMITHSONIA . . . Purchased in 1752 by Colonel Fielding Lewis, later owned by Dr. John Sutherland, then Dr. Hugh Mercer. Inherited by Ann Gordon Mercer Patton who donated it in 1808 to the Presbyterian Church. Present structure, erected in 1834, was used as a hospital during the Civil War. The name was given after 1865 when Miss Rebecca Smith, a much beloved local figure, was headmistress of the Assembly's Home and School.

PRINCE FREDERICK ARMS . . . The original house, erected in the late 1700s burned in 1807. Rebuilt in 1815 by Mayor Robert Mackay, it was referred to as "Mackay's Folly" as he overextended himself financially in its construction. Purchased two years later by Thomas Seddon, one of whose sons, James Seddon, became Secretary of War to the Confederate States of America.

# Stafford Heritage

THE boundaries of Maryland and Virginia were not yet definitely drawn in 1647 when Giles Brent moved across the river from Maryland to settle on a new plantation which he named "Peace". He had emigrated from England, son of an old Somerset family of the Catholic persuasion, and had served in various provincial offices for eight years preceding his move. His marriage to Kittamaquad, daughter of the Indian Emperor of Piscataway, incurred the wrath of his cousin, Lord Baltimore, when Brent laid claim to half of Maryland on his wife's behalf.

In 1648 the Virginia government formed the county of Northumberland which encompassed the entire Northern Neck within its bounds. Three years later Giles Brent took out his first land patent, as did his sisters, Margaret and Mary, who had followed him across the river. The three thus established the first Catholic settlement in the state. They settled on the prominent point later called Marlborough after the Duke of the same name. "Colonel Brent's" was the last stop for pioneers moving up the river to settle in the wilderness to the north. Margaret Brent was an outstanding woman of her time, intelligent and very much interested in the workings of laws and government. She was the first woman in the New World to ask for "voyce and vote allso", anticipating women's suffrage in this country by one hundred and seventy years. She was referred to in the Maryland courts as "Margaret Brent, Gent."

George Brent, nephew of the first three Brents, obtained a grant of 30,000 acres from James II in 1687 and was promised religious freedom. The next year the Reverend John Waugh, minister of the Aquia Episcopal Church, led an anti-Catholic crusade, assisted by Burr Harrison, John West and many of the settlers who were nervous about Indian attacks and were easily upset by rumors that the Catholics were planning a Protestant massacre with Indian assistance. People took up arms on both sides of the river but the Brents were highly respected by government leaders of the time and Council members Spencer, Allerton and Lee. These three arrested the ringleaders Waugh, Harrison and West and exacted public apologies from them.

The town of Stafford was created in 1715 as the county seat, and Falmouth was chartered in 1727 at the same time as Fredericksburg, and grew rapidly as did her sister town as an import-export center for lands as far west as the Blue Ridge Mountains.

The Reverend Alexander Scott was minister of Overwharton parish for twenty-seven years beginning in 1711, during which time he built a home on the present site of Quantico and called it "Dipple". He acquired thousands of acres of land over the years which were inherited by his younger brother, the Reverend James Scott, who later moved to Westwood, which was across Quantico Creek in Prince William County. The well-loved Reverend John Moncure succeeded Alexander Scott as minister and was responsible for the building in 1757 of the beautiful Aquia Church which is still standing.

At the time of the Battle of Fredericksburg, during the Civil War, Falmouth was headquarters for the Federal Army. After the withdrawal of troops from the bloody battle which took place across the river in December, 1862, the Army of the Potomac (Union) attempted to get around Lee's Confederate Army of Northern Virginia by fording the Rappahannock but a cloudburst bogged the effort down in a muddy mire and the offensive had to be abandoned.

Three courthouse sites have been in use since the county's formation. The first was on Marlborough Point, the second near the present boundary line of King George and Stafford Counties, marked only by the "Courthouse Spring", and the third, where the present building was erected in 1922, although Stafford town has been the county seat since 1715.

Because of its proximity to Fredericksburg and the building of Route 95 to Washington, the rural county is rapidly becoming urban. Youbedamn Point, once the terminus of the Richmond, Fredericksburg and Potomac Railroad where freighters were loaded at the large dock, is now the Aqua-Po Recreation Area. Quantico, which was a naval base during the Revolutionary War, servicing the "Potomac Navy", became a permanent installation for the Marine Corps in 1918.

CHATHAM . . . Built in 1769 by William Fitzhugh on land inherited from his great-grandfather, it was named in honor of the Earl of Chatham, an ardent advocate of American independence. The estate was famous for its private racetrack, its thoroughbreds, and its hospitality. Because of the strain of constant entertaining, living on the main road from Williamsburg to Alexandria, he finally retired to his inherited "Ravensworth" estate in Fairfax County.

CARLTON . . . This large frame house on a hilltop overlooks the village of Falmouth. It was built by John Short, (1763-1794) a merchant. A handsome staircase dominates the central hall; the balistrade ends in a ram's horn design. It was for many years after his death the home of his widow, Mrs. Judith (Ball) Short and was acquired in 1837 by John M. O'Bannon and occupied by his family for more than one hundred years.

CLEARVIEW . . . Built in 1750; it has a commanding view of Falmouth, the Rappahannock River, and Fredericksburg. Purchased in 1786 by Major Andrew Buchanan of General Washington's staff. At the time of the Civil War the owner was Thomas C. Scott.

# FALMOUTH

BELMONT . . . Built about 1761 by John Richards for his daughter, Mrs. Horner. Upon the death of William Knox of "Windsor Lodge" in Culpeper County, it became in 1805 the home of his widow, Mrs. Susannah Stuart (Fitzhugh) Knox (1751-1823). The mansion was in recent years the home of Mr. and Mrs. Gari Melchers, both deceased, and was bequeathed by the latter on her death to the State of Virginia as an art museum.

— 17 —

AQUIA CHURCH . . .
Serving Overwharton Parish, which was established before 1680, and replacing a church built in 1751 which burned three years later, the present church was erected in 1757. It has a rare triple-deck pulpit. The Reverend John Moncure, rector from 1738 to 1764, is buried beneath a stone bearing the inscription: "In memory of the Race of the House of Moncure".

UNION METHODIST CHURCH . . . At Falmouth, on a hill above the river east of the highway stands a church facade and tower of sturdy brick, but no church building remains. This church was probably the outgrowth of Greaves' Chapel, founded by the Reverend Moncure Daniel Conway, first a Methodist minister and later a leading Unitarian pastor in Victorian London.

EASTWOOD MANOR...
This house was built in 1820 by John Gray on property owned by his family from the 1700's, and it has remained in the family's possession ever since. Six miles east of Fredericksburg.

POTOMAC CREEK BRIDGE...
Built during the Civil War by
Federal troops in nine days from
standing timber: called the "bean-
pole and cornstalk bridge."

OLD JAIL . . . Probably built about 1785 at
Stafford Courthouse, and destroyed about 1922 when
a new brick courthouse was erected. The worn steps
indicate heavy traffic.

CHOPAWAMSIC BAPTIST
CHURCH . . . Near the site of
Quantico, this church was built in
1766, but demolished many years
ago. The quaint photograph was
taken before 1900.

# Prince William County's Potomac Area

ALTHOUGH John Smith ascended the Potomac to the falls in 1608, settlers did not follow him until nearly fifty years later. Thomas Burbage took out the first patent in the Occoquan area in 1653. This land was eventually acquired by George Mason II, grandfather of George Mason IV of Gunston Hall.

The vast acreage of the "Leesylvania" plantation which lies between Neabsco and Powell Creeks was patented in 1658 by Gervais Dobson, who shortly conveyed it to Councillor Henry Corbin of Pecatone Plantation in Westmoreland County. Corbin willed it to his daughter Laetitia, in 1675, the year following her marriage to Richard Lee II, son of Richard Lee, the emigrant. Their grandson Henry Lee II inherited the plantation and was the first member of the family to reside on the land which had belonged to the family for four generations. He moved there in 1753 with his bride, Lucy Grymes, who had been unsuccessfully wooed by George Washington.

Among their children born at Leesylvania were Colonel Henry III ("Light-Horse Harry") Lee, Governor of Virginia, and father of Robert E. Lee; Attorney General Charles Lee; Representative Richard Bland Lee; and Edmund Jennings Lee, Mayor of Alexandria.

In 1681 the General Assembly directed the establishment of a ferry on the Occoquan, which in 1744 was noted as being operated between the lands of Anne Mason and the village of Colchester.

When deposits of supposed copper ore were found in 1728 on Frying Pan Run in what was later to become Fairfax County, Robert "King" Carter formed a mining company. When Thomas Lee refused to let him cross his lands to bring the copper ore to tidewater below Little Falls, Carter opened up the Ox Road from the Occoquan to the mine and erected warehouses at Colchester. The new road ran past Payne's Church and the present site of the Fairfax Courthouse up to Frying Pan Run, a tributary of Horsepen Run. Although the "copper ore" turned out to be green sandstone, the opening of this road was of primary importance to the future development of the interior lands of the upper Northern Neck.

In 1749 Charles Ewell of Bel Air planned an ironworks on the Occoquan. This plan reached fruition in 1755 when John Ballendine was offered financial backing by John Tayloe and Presley Thornton, owners of the ironworks already in existence on Neabsco Creek. A partnership was formed and by 1759 Occoquan was a manufacturing town with mills, stores and warehouses. The most impressive home was Ballendine's "Rockledge". It was designed by William Buckland who did the interiors of Gunston Hall and was the architect of many of the finest homes of this section of Virginia. It is still a handsome edifice perched on a rock ledge, commanding a fine view.

In 1759 Archdeacon Burnaby described the community as follows:

"About two miles above Colchester, there is an iron furnace, a forge, two saw mills and a bolting mill. At our return we had an opportunity of visiting them. They have every convenience of wood and water that can be wished for. The ore wrought here is brought from Maryland: not that there is any doubt of there being enough in the adjacent hills, but the inhabitants are discouraged from trying for it by the proprietor's (Lord Fairfax) having reserved to himself a third of all ore that may be discovered in the Northern Neck."

Ballendine, Tayloe and Thornton dissolved their partnership in 1760 and the owner of Rockledge became so hard-pressed that he had to borrow money from John Semple of Maryland. In 1762, Ballendine turned his holdings over to Semple, who abandoned the ironworks in favor of flour mills. The ironworks at Neabsco continued in operation until after the Revolution.

Nathaniel Ellicott, a Quaker, bought the flour mills in 1800 and employed John Davis, who was an English novelist and traveler, as a tutor for his children. The author wrote in the following year:

"Occoquan consists only of a house built upon a rock, three others on the riverside and a half dozen log huts scattered at some distance. Yet no place can be more romantic than the view of Occoquan to a stranger, after crossing the rustic bridge which has been constructed by the inhabitants across the stream. He contemplates the river urging its course along the mountains that lose themselves among the clouds: he beholds vessels taking on board flour from the mills, and others, deeply laden, expanding their sails to the breeze, while every face wears contentment, every gale wafts health, and echo from the rocks multiplies the voice of the waggoners calling to their teams."

By 1828, Nathaniel and Samuel Janney were operating the mills, and in Joseph Martin's "Gazetteer of Virginia, 1835", the following was recorded regarding Occoquan:

"The town contains about 50 dwelling houses, several mercantile stores and various mechanics, a cotton manufactory in complete operation and one of the first established in the State, now running 1,000 spindles, an extensive manufacturing flour mill grinding in the ordinary season 150 barrels per day, with the necessary appendages of grist, saw and plaster mills. A handsome and permanent bridge is erected across the river at this place; over the bridge and through the town runs the great mail route from Washington to the South. The principal trade of the town is with the counties of Fairfax and Fauquier . . . This village is in a flourishing condition and with confidence looks forward to further improvement."

The promising future was not realized. Silt washing down Occoquan Creek from extensive clearing and tobacco farming on the lands above filled up the channel and ships were no longer able to reach the mills at Occoquan.

The town of Dumfries on Quantico Creek was organized in 1749 by Scottish merchants from Glasgow. It was named after a Scottish town south of Glasgow. One of the merchants, John Carlyle, later became a man of importance in Alexandria. Although England had tried to maintain a trade monopoly with the Colonies in order to collect the customs and market the commodities at home, the merchants of Scotland eventually gained access to America, established businesses there and became landholders. The secret of their success was the fact that they were, by inclination and training, prudent and economical in managing their businesses. They offered the planters higher prices for their tobacco and other products. These Scottish merchants recognized the importance of access to the interior Piedmont lands and encouraged the building of roads. They also estab-

BEL AIR . . . Built in 1740 by Charles Ewell, it was also the home of his son, Colonel Jesse Ewell of the Revolution and of "Parson" Mason Locke Weems, his son-in-law, who was the first biographer of George Washington. One of the chimneys has a base measurement of nearly twenty feet. Located seven miles west of Dumfries.

DUMFRIES HOTEL . . . Erected about 1760 by George Williams, it was first known as Williams' Ordinary, then as Love's Tavern and later as the Stage Coach Inn. It is architecturally notable for the stone quoins at the corners and around the doorway.

lished stores at strategic points, such as the "Red Store" around which the town of Warrenton developed.

Many prominent families south of Dumfries saw the possibilities of a bright future for the town and numerous lots were purchased by absentee landowners as investments. Taverns were built and their prices were carefully regulated by the court to protect residents and transients who frequented the busy port town.

Alexander Henderson, who came from Scotland in 1756 and settled in Colchester, was the founder of the American "chain-store" system. He then moved to Dumfries where he was so successful with his store that he opened branches at Colchester, Occoquan and Alexandria. His home, built in 1785, is the only remaining early building in Dumfries besides the Stage Coach Inn. The Tobacco Inspector's House, built in 1690, was the oldest structure in Prince William County until it collapsed in 1963. Its most unusual feature was the mock-

stone exterior similar to that of Mount Vernon.

Dumfries was a one-product town—tobacco. When the American Revolution deprived the merchants in Scotland of American tobacco, they turned to the West Indies for sugar. Meanwhile, Quantico Creek silted up so badly that ships were unable to reach Dumfries which gradually became a ghost town. Ambitious merchants and professional men left to seek their fortunes elsewhere, particularly in Alexandria. James Madison is quoted as having commented in 1827 the following regarding pre-Revolutionary conditions:

"Scotch merchants in Virginia used to have a meeting twice a year to decide on the rate of exchange, the price of tobacco and the advances on the prices of their goods. This was the substantial legislation of the colony."

For the history of the development of the Piedmont section of Prince William County, please refer to page 178.

PRINCE WILLIAM FOREST PARK . . .
This reservation of 12,290 acres extends on
the east side from Triangle and Dumfries,
northwestward nine miles to Independent
Hill. There are eighty-nine identified
species of trees and shrubs, and a variety
of wildlife.

WILDERNESS TRAIL . . . Here man is the guest and nature
the host.

CAMPING . . . Throughout the year the
National Park Service provides a Headquarters Office and Nature Center, camp-
ground, and a trailer village.

RIPPON LODGE . . . Designed and built about 1725 by Colonel Richard Blackburn of Ripon, in Yorkshire, England, on part of the Burbage Grant of 1653. Blackburn was the architect or master builder of the oldest part of Mount Vernon and the first Falls Church. Two of his descendants became mistresses of Mount Vernon; Julia Anne, as Mrs. Bushrod Washington, and Jane Charlotte, as Mrs. John Augustine Washington. Sketches made in 1796 by Benjamin Latrobe, architect of the Capitol at Washington, when he was a visitor at Rippon Lodge, show another house about thirty-five yards to the east. A notation states that this house "must have been built near a hundred years ago, for the oldest people now living do not remember when nor by whom it was built."

LEESYLVANIA . . . Site of the ancestral home of Robert E. Lee's branch of the family where his grandparents, Henry Lee II and Lucy Grymes Lee lie buried. The plantation home burned about 1790. The estate was sold to Henry Fairfax in 1825, whose family lived there in a home which may have pre-dated the Lee residence. The Fairfax home burned in 1910 and the ruins of the walls and a chimney are all that remain.

ROCKLEDGE . . . Under the supervision of the noted architect, William Buckland, this house was erected in 1758 for John Ballendine, early industrialist, mapmaker, and a founder of Occoquan.

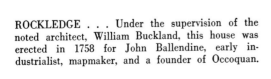

# Fairfax County's Potomac Area

THE early Potomac plantations were self-contained communities whereupon were provided most of the necessities of life and some of the luxuries. We are fortunate to have an accurate contemporary description of a typical gentleman's estate, Gunston Hall of Fairfax County.

Following is an excerpt from an article, "The Historic Potomac River", by William Edgar Rogers, from the publications of the Columbia Historical Society.

"In the life of George Mason of Gunston Hall, his son gives an exceedingly interesting account of the manner of living on one of these great plantations.

'It was very much the practice,' he wrote, 'with gentle men of landed and slave estates in the interior of Virginia, so to organize them as to have considerable resources within themselves; to employ and pay but few tradesmen and to buy little or none of the coarse stuffs and materials used by them, and this practice became stronger and more general during the long period of the Revolutionary War which in a great measure cut off the means of supply from elsewhere. Thus my father had among his slaves, carpenters, coopers, sawyers, blacksmiths, tanners, curriers, shoemakers, spinners, weavers and knitters, and even a distiller.

'The woods furnished timber and plank for the carpenter and coopers and charcoal for the blacksmith; his cattle killed for his own consumption and for sale, supplied skins for the tanners, curriers and shoemakers, and his sheep gave wool and his fields produced cotton and flax for the weavers and spinners, and his orchards fruit for the distillery. His carpenters and sawyers built and kept in repair all of the dwelling houses, barns, stables, ploughs, harrows, gates, etc. on the plantations and outhouses and at the home house. His cooper made the hogsheads the tobacco was prized in and the tight casks to hold the cider and other liquors; the tanners and curriers with the proper vats tanned and dressed the skins as well for upper as lower leather to the full amount of the consumption of the estate and the shoemakers made them into shoes for the negroes.

'A professed shoemaker was hired for three months in the year to make up the shoes for the white part of the family. The blacksmiths did all of the iron work required by the establishment and the spinners and weavers made all the coarse cloth and stockings used by the negroes, and some of the finer texture worn by the white family. The distiller made every fall a good deal of peach, apple and persimmon brandy. All the beeves and hogs for consumption and sale were driven up there and slaughtered at the proper season. My father had in his service a white man, a weaver of fine stuffs to weave himself and superintend the black weavers and a white woman to superintend the negro spinning women.'

George Mason directed his younger brother, Thomson, to bring back from England a "joiner" who would help to finish the interior work of Gunston Hall. Young William Buckland was selected. He had been apprenticed to his uncle James, a master joiner who was also proprietor of a book store on Pater Noster Row which specialized in the sale of architectural folios. Young Buckland's later work shows that he made good use of his opportunities. There is evidence that in addition to Gunston Hall he also worked on others including Rockledge, Mount Airy, Nomini, and many beautiful homes in Annapolis, the foremost being the Hammond Harwood House. Of his great talent, a contemporary said, "There was no taste in Annapolis until William Buckland came."

For the history of the development of the Piedmont section of Fairfax County, please refer to page 62.

LAZY SUSAN INN . . . A charming restaurant high on King's House Hill where once stood an Indian longhouse, overlooking Occoquan Creek, Belmont Bay and the Potomac River. Here one may dine in the Virginia tradition surrounded by examples of Colonial life and fine antiques.

FAIRFAX ARMS . . . Also known as "Colchester Inn" this famous ordinary was built in 1750. About 180 John Davis wrote, "Every luxury that money can purchase is to be obtained at first summons . . . The riche viands cover the table . . . and ice cools the Madeira . . Apartments are numerous and at the same time spaciou . . . Carpets of delicate texture cover the floor; ar glasses are suspended from the walls in which a Goliat might survey himself."

GUNSTON HALL . . . Home of George Mason, author of the Virginia Declaration of Rights, on which was patterned the Constitution's first ten amendments. Louis Hertle, who died in 1949, willed the property to the State of Virginia, under the custody of The National Society of Colonial Dames of America, who have restored, furnished and operated Gunston Hall as a museum house in honor of George Mason.

THE GARDEN . . . The deer park extended from the prominence upon which the house stood to the Potomac some distance away. The boxwood hedge planted by George Mason, is one of the finest in the world. The formal garden has been restored by The Garden Club of Virginia.

PALADIAN ROOM . . . The home was erected 1755-58, with the interior and porches designed by William Buckland whom George Mason's brother, Thomson had brought from England under indenture.

POHICK CHURCH . . . Erected 1769 to replace an earlier wooden structure which stood two miles south. George Washington, George William Fairfax, and George Mason were vestrymen and members of the building committee. The Reverend Lee Massey was their pastor; his tombstone is now inside the Church, his remains beneath the pulpit.

EARLY GRAVES . . . Aside is shown an old gravestone from Prince William County. Another old stone is that of William Herris, brought from the Leesylvania estate. From the "Summer Hill" plantation of the Alexander family, now the National Airport site, came the tombstone of "Long Tom", a treacherous Indian who was killed while ambushing a member of the family.

ARCH HALL . . . Erected 1796 in Alexandria on the corner of Franklin and Columbus Street, as a townhouse for Nelly Custis of Woodlawn. Later disfigured with Victorian gingerbread, it was restored in 1936 by Dr. and Mrs. Ford Swetnam. In 1950, to save it from destruction in a business area, Everett L. Lommasson had it carefully dismantled and reconstructed on the shores of Belmont Bay.

MASON NECK . . . The sylvan peninsula was part of the vast Gunston Hall estate. George Mason's son John, in 1832, described the area ". . . the native deer had been preserved there in abundance from the first settlement . . . The land was elevated some twenty feet above the surface of the river, with the exception of one extensive marsh and three or four water courses . . . about two-thirds of it were yet clothed with the primitive wood." Negotiations are under way to preserve this wilderness-wildlife area for posterity.

GREENWAY COURT DEPENDENCY . . . All that remains of the manor complex established in the Shenandoah Valley in 1748 by Thomas, Sixth Lord Fairfax, Proprietor of the "Northern Neck", where he resided until his death in 1781. This small building was used as the Land Office where he collected quitrents.

BELVOIR . . . On the precipitous banks of the Potomac, are the foundations of the mansion erected about 1741 by William Fairfax, patron of George Washington. Belvoir was inherited in 1757 by his son, Colonel George William Fairfax, who returned to England in 1773 upon falling heir to the ancestral estates there. The mansion was partially destroyed by fire ten years later, and the remaining walls demolished by British guns during the War of 1812.

BELVOIR ON THE POTOMACK

WOODLAWN . . . This late Georgian style mansion, completed in 1805, was designed by William Thornton, first architect of the Capitol. The two thousand acre plantation, cut by George Washington from the Mount Vernon estate, was a wedding gift to Martha's granddaughter, Nelly Custis, upon her marriage to his nephew, Lawrence Lewis. The wedding took place at Mount Vernon on Washington's last living birthday, February 22, 1799.

THE MUSIC ROOM . . . As was the custom in Colonial and Early Federal times, music played an important part in the life of the Lewis family. The Lewis girls all sang, played the harp and the pianoforte, instructed by their accomplished mother. Woodlawn is owned by the National Trust for Historic Preservation.

POPE-LEIGHEY HOUSE . . . Architect Frank Lloyd Wright designed this modern American home in which man would not be removed from the out-of-doors, but sheltered in a structure which would make him aware of the freedom of space with a relationship to nature. He termed this style the Natural or Usonian House, from which many contemporary architectural concepts have grown. The Pope-Leighey House, named for two consecutive owners, was erected in 1940 in Falls Church. To avoid its destruction in the path of Route 66, it was presented to the National Trust for Historic Preservation and relocated on the grounds of Woodlawn Plantation.

MOUNT VERNON . . . The home and plantation of George and Martha Washington, where they raised Martha's son John, and daughter Patsy who died at the age of 17. John Parke Custis married Eleanor Calvert of Maryland. He died of "camp fever" at Yorktown in 1781, leaving four young children, two of whom the Washingtons adopted and raised. One was George Washington Parke Custis who later built Arlington House, the other was Eleanor (Nelly) who became the mistress of Woodlawn. The home and plantation were saved for posterity through the efforts of Ann Pamela Cunningham of South Carolina who in 1853 organized The Mount Vernon Ladies' Association which acquired and has since maintained the property.

CENTRAL HALL . . . The most comfortable part of the house during warm weather, with large doors to the courtyard and piazza, where much informal social life centered.

WASHINGTON'S GRIST MILL . . . The original mill was constructed by Augustine Washington, mentioned in his will 1743, and completely rebuilt by George in 1759. Of great interest to him, he visited it on his last ride before his death. The present structure is a reproduction erected on the site in 1932 by the State of Virginia, the earlier structure having fallen into ruin about 1850.

WELLINGTON . . . Once a part of the Mount Vernon estate, the house was probably built by William Clifton before 1750. Tobias Lear, secretary to George Washington and tutor of his adopted children, leased the home and three hundred and sixty acres from Washington, who later bequeathed them to him for a life interest. After his death in 1816 the farm, which had become known as Walnut Tree Farm, reverted to Washington heirs.

MOUNT VERNON MEMORIAL PARKWAY . . . The Parkway extends from Mount Vernon to the Arlington Memorial Bridge, where it connects with the George Washington Memorial Parkway which continues up the Palisades to Cabin John Bridge. Both are under the jurisdiction of the National Park Service.

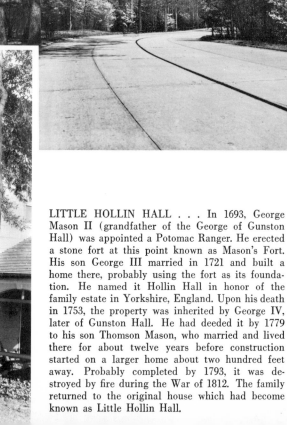

LITTLE HOLLIN HALL . . . In 1693, George Mason II (grandfather of the George of Gunston Hall) was appointed a Potomac Ranger. He erected a stone fort at this point known as Mason's Fort. His son George III married in 1721 and built a home there, probably using the fort as its foundation. He named it Hollin Hall in honor of the family estate in Yorkshire, England. Upon his death in 1753, the property was inherited by George IV, later of Gunston Hall. He had deeded it by 1779 to his son Thomson Mason, who married and lived there for about twelve years before construction started on a larger home about two hundred feet away. Probably completed by 1793, it was destroyed by fire during the War of 1812. The family returned to the original house which had become known as Little Hollin Hall.

FORT HUNT . . . Established 1897 as a Coast Artillery Battery for the proposed Potomac Defenses of Washington at the time of the Spanish-American War. Named by President McKinley to honor General Henry Hunt, Chief of Artillery at the Battles of Fredericksburg and Gettysburg, who later became Commander of the Old Soldiers' Home in Washington. It is now a recreation center and headquarters for the National Capital Park Police.

PARKWAY CEDARS . . . Throughout the Virginia countryside, one sees rows of cedar trees, some along fences and others across fields marking the sites of former fences. These trees are gifts of the mocking birds whose favorite berries are cedar, and whose frequent perches are fences.

COLLINGWOOD . . . Today one may enjoy a fine meal in this stately mansion which was constructed in 1785 upon the River Farm portion of George Washington's estate. Collingwood derived its name from the British Admiral who was the hero of the Battle of Trafalgar when he assumed command of the Fleet upon the death of Lord Nelson. Nearby still pours from the hillside the fine spring which the Indians called The Great Fountain to which Washington refers in his diary as the Johnson Spring. English sailing vessels filled their casks there on their homeward journeys. Probably the location of both the home and the Clifton Ferry crossing here were determined by the excellent supply of cold sweet water. Nearby was also a duelling ground, the last duel reported to have been fought there in 1805.

# Alexandria Heritage

A grant of 6,000 acres was made in October, 1669 by Sir William Berkeley, Governor of Virginia to Robert Howson. The land lay between "My Lord's Island" (now Theodore Roosevelt Island) and "English Indian Cabin Creek" (now Hunting Creek) and included the site of the present City of Alexandria as well as a strip about three miles wide extending up the Potomac to include what is now the Arlington National Cemetery. In less than a month the Howson patent was conveyed to John Alexander for six hogsheads of tobacco.

In 1730 a warehouse was authorized by Governor William Gooch's tobacco inspection act. A site was selected on the north side of Great Hunting Creek. James Pagan and William Ramsay of Scotland, and John Carlyle, recently of Dumfries, established residences near the warehouse about 1740. A town was laid out and chartered as Alexandria in 1749, named after the family on whose land it was established. A proposal to change the name to "Belhaven" was rejected by the Assembly in 1752.

George Washington helped to survey the streets, the first of which were named after royalty, the newer streets after American patriots as the town grew. The sandstone curbing was brought from Aquia Creek quarries, and bricks, cobble, and flagstones were used for pavement.

Built as it was on the main river rather than on a creek, Alexandria was not plagued with the siltation problems which slowly strangled Dumfries, Occoquan and Colchester. Roads and then turnpikes were built in order to draw commerce from the growing Piedmont areas. Taverns were built, shipbuilding became an industry, and boats laden with commodities from distant ports unloaded their wares and sailed away laden with flour, wheat, and tobacco grown as far away as the Shenandoah Valley.

When General Edward Braddock stopped here to assemble his troops for the ill-fated campaign to Fort Duquesne in 1755, in the French and Indian War, five Royal Governors met with him in the Carlyle House and agreed to get their legislatures to levy war taxes to support the effort.

Justice George Johnston was credited by Thomas Jefferson with the constitutional argument embodied in the resolution on the Stamp Act which Patrick Henry offered in Williamsburg in May, 1765. Because Washington, Mason and Johnston were co-workers for many years in the causes of justice and freedom, they have often been referred to as "The Three Georges".

In July, 1774 George Washington presided in the courthouse at a meeting to elect delegates to the first Virginia Convention and to protest against the Boston Port Bill. The Fairfax Resolves, drawn by George Mason of Gunston Hall, and adopted at this meeting, stated Virginia's position on the Crown, Parliament and taxation, and suggested cooperation between the colonies on a united platform.

After the Revolutionary War, Alexandria experienced a great surge of building in anticipation of becoming a large center of commerce, but Baltimore and Georgetown emerged as strong contenders.

There were also the housekeeping chores illustrated by the passing of a variety of statutes. About 1790 lotteries were authorized by the General Assembly for the paving of streets and the building of a church for the use of members of the Presbyterian Society. Problems of the standardizing of measurements led in part to the establishment of official hay weighing scales in 1798, the same year that the Alexandria Library Company was incorporated. An ordinance passed in 1802 treats with another subject and reads as follows, "Whereas, a considerable portion of the housekeepers of Alexandria, for the more convenient furnishing of milk to their families, are in the habit of maintaining cows; and whereas, a supply of this useful article from that source must be precarious unless males be provided to range with the herds . . ." The Council immediately purchased two town bulls and put a person in charge of each one.

There was great celebration in the town in 1824 when General Lafayette made his famous visit. On this occasion the Frenchman offered the following toast: "To the City of Alexandria; may her prosperity and happiness more and more realize the fondest hopes of our venerated Washington!"

Alexandria was ceded to the District of Columbia in 1789, but Congress did not take control of the District until 1800. In 1814, the British sailed two frigates into the harbor, marched through the silent streets to the Town Hall, and left the belligerent populace the poorer by 16,000 barrels of flour, 1,000 hogsheads of tobacco, several ships and other items including 5,000 barrels of wine.

Alexandria desired retrocession to Virginia in order to share in the great expansion of internal communications then in progress in Virginia. As part of the District of Columbia, Alexandria received no consideration from Virginia.

After the retrocession by Congress in 1846 Alexandria enjoyed a great boom and became an important railroad center. Alexandria capital built the Orange and Alexandria Railroad which was extended to Lynchburg and connected with the Virginia and Tennessee Railroad across the state to Memphis. Locomotives for these and other railroads were built in Alexandria. The town's prosperity as a commercial and industrial center seemed assured until the Civil War intervened and left it bankrupt.

Alexandria went into a slump which was reversed at the time of World War I when shipbuilding was resumed and the growth of the Federal District across the river brought in many new residents.

Maps of the City are available at the Alexandria Tourist Bureau and the Alexandria Chamber of Commerce.

EARLY VIEW OF ALEXANDRIA

RAMSAY HOUSE . . . Constructed about 1750 by William Ramsay, one of the founders of Alexandria, it is reputed to have been the earliest building in the city. Washington noted in his diary that he attended Ramsay's funeral in 1785. The house was restored in 1956, and is the headquarters of the Alexandria Tourist Council. The Hunting Creek Garden Club restored the garden. King and Fairfax Streets.

CARLYLE HOUSE . . . The Scottish merchant John Carlyle, who, like William Ramsay was a founder of the town, erected this residence in 1752. In 1755, General Braddock met here with five Colonial governors to plan his ill-fated campaign against the French and Indians. Twenty-three year old George Washington was a member of his staff. Massive masonry beneath the house is said to have been an older foundation of a fortification against Indians. A stone-lined tunnel originally led down to the wharves. 123 North Fairfax Street.

FRIENDSHIP FIRE COMPANY . . . In 1752 a town ordinance decreed that all wooden chimneys be replaced by brick or stone. The first fire company in Alexandria was organized in 1774. Now a museum, the most cherished possession is a seven-foot hand-pumper fire engine presented in 1794 by George Washington, which he had purchased for four hundred dollars in Philadelphia. As the volunteer fire companies were presented bonuses when they saved insured property, a metal "fire mark" plate was placed on the front of each insured building. As other fire companies were established, competition became keen for the awards. The design of the Friendship Fire Company's fire mark is duplicated in its weather vane. 107 South Alfred Street.

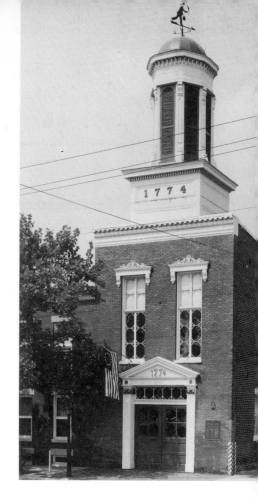

THE ATHENEUM . . . This fine example of the Greek Revival phase of neoclassic architecture was erected in the mid-1800s by the Bank of the Old Dominion. It was later used as a Free Methodist Church until purchased in 1964 by the Northern Virginia Fine Arts Association for their headquarters and gallery. Northwest corner of Prince and Lee Streets.

LYCEUM HALL . . . Erected about 1840 by the Lyceum Society as a lecture hall and to house the Alexandria Library, which had been in operation for fifty years. The Federal forces used the building as a hospital during the Civil War. 201 South Washington Street.

THE CANNON FOUNTAIN . . . Near Gadsby's Tavern stands a drinking fountain, the central standard of which is one of General Braddock's cannon, several of which were abandoned when they proved too heavy to pull over the rough trails en route to Fort Duquesne. The fountain provides water at three levels; a spout and bowl for birds at the top, below which are dolphin spouts for man and a trough for horses, with a bowl at the base for dogs and cats.

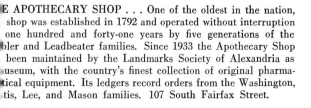

E APOTHECARY SHOP . . . One of the oldest in the nation, shop was established in 1792 and operated without interruption one hundred and forty-one years by five generations of the bler and Leadbeater families. Since 1933 the Apothecary Shop been maintained by the Landmarks Society of Alexandria as useum, with the country's finest collection of original pharma-tical equipment. Its ledgers record orders from the Washington, tis, Lee, and Mason families. 107 South Fairfax Street.

GADSBY'S TAVERN . . . The two-story "City Tavern" was erected in 1752 by Charles Mason, "Taylor"; the adjacent three-story building by John Wise in 1792 who operated the latter until 1796 when it was leased to John Gadsby who operated both properties until the summer of 1808. Here George Washington is said to have recruited his first command in 1754. The Tavern has been a mecca for social life in Alexandria for three centuries. The Garden Club of Virginia restored the courtyard. Many patriotic organizations and local civic and cultural groups have assisted the American Legion Post 24 in restoring and maintaining the two buildings. 128 North Royal Street.

FLOUNDER HOUSE . . . Leased in 1779 by executors of John Alexander to Colonel John Fitzgerald and Valentine Peers at a price which indicated that the house was standing thereon at that time. Peers assigned his equity to Fitzgerald in 1784. Fitzgerald was Mayor of Alexandria, 1792-1794. John Roberts, who was Mayor and official host of Lafayette in 1824, had resided there the two years previous, then moved to the north side of the 700 block of King Street. The Flounder House is an excellent example of a type of architecture unique to Alexandria. 317 South Saint Asaph Street.

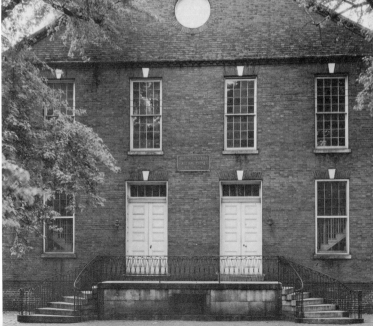

CHRIST CHURCH . . . The land was given by the Alexander family. Construction of the church began in 1767, upon a design by the architect of the Falls Church, Colonel James Wren, and was completed in 1773. Wren also lettered The Lord's Prayer, The Creed and The Ten Commandments on wooden panels on each side of the wine-glass pulpit. Here George Washington owned a pew and Robert E. Lee was confirmed. Cameron and Columbus Streets.

PRESBYTERIAN MEETING HOUSE . . . Erection started in 1767, building completed in 1774 by John Carlyle, rebuilt in the 1830s following a fire. Buried here are the remains of the "Unknown Soldier of the Revolutionary War" as well as many famous patriots. 321 South Fairfax Street.

NORFORD INN . . . Alexandria was noted for its many taverns, including the Norford Inn. The present building ... erected about 1815 and has been operated continuously ... an inn. The courtyard with its Old World atmosphere ... inds one of the French Quarter at New Orleans. 311 ... neron Street.

LAFAYETTE HOUSE . . . This house, erected in 1815 with excellent architectural detail, was loaned to Lafayette and his staff in 1824 by Mrs. Thomas Lawrason. Upon his departure, the city presented her with a silver cup created by an Alexandria silversmith, William A. Williams, in appreciation of her generous hospitality. 301 South Saint Asaph Street.

THE OLD CLUB . . . The local tradition is that the oldest portion was originally built at Broomilaw Point on the Potomac nearby, as a clubhouse by a company of gentlemen including George Washington and George Mason. It was moved to the present site about 1790. Thomas White acquired the property in 1793, and many additions were made in the one hundred and twenty-five years of the family's occupancy. The valued furniture was boxed and buried in the garden when the British threatened invasion of Alexandria in 1814. Another delightful place to dine in traditional atmosphere. 555 South Washington Street.

HOME OF GEORGE WILLIAM FAIRFAX . . . William Fairfax purchased this lot about 1750. He and his son, George William Fairfax were among the trustees and founders of Alexandria, members of the House of Burgesses, and the Council. At one time it was owned briefly by Robert Adam, founder of the Masonic Lodge of Alexandria. It was acquired in 1790 by William Hodgson, who married Portia Lee and was later occupied by her sister Cornelia, who married John Hopkins, both husbands being prominent in Alexandria business circles. 207 Prince Street.

HOME OF LORD FAIRFAX . . . At least some portion of this fine house was existing in 1795 when James Irvin purchased the property from Charles Alexander, who two months later sold it to Leven and Suzanne Powell who resided there for two years. William Yeaton, a ship designer from New England, purchased it in 1797 and completed it with fine architectural details, but overextended his credit and lost the property in 1816. Some years later, Thomas, Lord Fairfax Ninth Baron of Cameron, acquired it as a winter residence and it remained in the family until 1875 when Doctor Orlando Fairfax sold it to David Windsor. It then came into the possession of the Crilly family from whom the present owners purchased it in 1962. 607 Cameron Street.

FAIRFAX HOUSE STAIRWAY

HOME OF DOCTOR DICK . . . Designated by the Chamber of Commerce plaque thereon as the residence of Doctor Elisha Cullen Dick, a Philadelphia Quaker who was health officer for Alexandria during the yellow fever epidemic. He served under "Lighthorse Harry" Lee in the 1794 Whisky Rebellion. In 1791, with George Washington, Doctor Dick laid the corner stone of the District of Columbia at Jones Point, in the capacity of Worshipful Master of the Alexandria Lodge of Masons. He was in consultation with Doctor Craik during Washington's last illness and conducted the Masonic service for the funeral. 209 Prince Street.

HOME OF DR. CRAIK . . . Built about 1790 for John Murray, this home was purchased in 1795 by Doctor James Craik, friend and family physician of George Washington. They were military associates in the French and Indian War and in the Continental Army. Washington willed Doctor Craik a tambour secretary and a circular chair which have been returned to Mount Vernon. 210 Duke Street.

HOME OF DOCTOR WILLIAM BROWN . . . Built prior to the Revolution on a lot purchased by Augustine Washington, brother of George, at the first auction of lots in 1749. The property passed through several owners before being bought in 1783 by Doctor William Brown. Washington appointed him Physician-General and Director of Hospitals of the Continental Army. In 1778, he wrote the first U.S. Pharmacopoeia, entirely in Latin. He was a charter member of the Society of the Cincinnati. He died in 1792 at the age of forty-two from hardships suffered at Valley Forge. Unique features of the house are the hand-hewn stone sink and large kitchen fireplace with original crane and oven. 212 South Fairfax Street.

HENRY LEE HOUSE . . . Erected in 1796, Henry Lee III ("Light-Horse Harry") brought his family to this home from Stratford in the summer of 1810, when Robert E. Lee was but three years old. 611 Cameron Street.

ROBERT E. LEE HOUSE . . . Built in 1795 by John Potts, it was purchased in 1799 by William Fitzhugh of Chatham as a town house while constructing a home on his Ravensworth estate. Here, on July 7, 1804, his only daughter, Mary Lee Fitzhugh, at the age of sixteen, married George Washington Parke Custis and became the mistress of Arlington House. Here Mrs. Henry Lee and her children resided from late 1811 to 1816 and from 1821 to 1825, during which time Robert E. Lee was prepared for West Point by Benjamin Hallowell, who at that time conducted his school next door. Open daily from 9 to 5. 607 Oronoco Street.

EDMUND JENNINGS LEE HOUSE . . . Built about 1800 by this distinguished attorney through whose efforts the Fairfax Glebe lands were saved from confiscation by the new government after the separation of Church and State following the American Revolution. Later, the sale of these lands defrayed the expense of erecting a steeple on Christ Church and the church-yard enclosure. 428 North Washington Street.

LLOYD HOUSE . . . Erected in 1793 by John Wise, a prominent citizen, it later became Benjamin Hallowell's School. In a few years, the house was purchased by John Lloyd upon his marriage to Anne Harriotte Lee, daughter of Edmund Jennings Lee. It remained in the family for nearly a century. 220 North Washington Street.

FENDALL-LEE HOUSE . . . Built in 1785 by Philip Richard Fendall, who frequently entertained the Washingtons in his house. His widow, Mary Lee Fendall, obtained 607 Oronoco Street for her sister-in-law, Mrs. Henry Lee, in 1811. Edmund Jennings Lee lived here from 1836 until his death in 1843.

STAIRWELL IN THE
FENDALL-LEE HOUSE . . .

**DENEALE HOUSE . . .** This house was reputedly erected by a wealthy New Englander as a wedding gift for his daughter upon her marriage to Captain George Deneale. He was the court clerk who recorded George Washington's will at the new Fairfax Courthouse in the town of Providence in 1800. 323 South Fairfax Street.

**GEORGE JOHNSTON HOUSE . . .** In 1757, Gentleman Justice George Johnston purchased this lot from Henry Fitzhugh and "caused to have built in that year a brick house, a livery, and a soigon (smokehouse)", upon moving from Winchester to Alexandria to serve as Presiding Justice of the Fairfax Court and Town Trustee. He also represented Fairfax County as a member of the House of Burgesses in Williamsburg, and took a prominent part in the revolt against the Stamp Act. He died in 1766 in the prime of life, but left two sons to take their part in the Revolution which resulted from this stand against British tyranny. This Alexandria house later became the home of Johnston's daughter Sarah and her husband, Colonel Robert Hanson Harrison, Washington's military secretary, who probably added the front portion of the house. Fragments of the original seawall remain in the rear of the garden. 224 South Lee Street.

**DULANY HOUSE . . .** Built in 1783 as a town house by Benjamin Dulany who had extensive holdings in Fairfax County. It was purchased in 1818 by Attorney Robert I. Taylor whose daughter Rosalie was one of the flower girls who escorted Lafayette through Alexandria in 1824. 601 Duke Street.

**THE WILLIAM FOWLE HOUSE**
. . . In 1797, James Patton bought a half-acre lot upon which he built a "flounder" house. In 1810, William Fowle, a prominent merchant who had recently come from Boston acquired this and adjoining property extending to Washington and King Streets, enlarged the house for his eighteen children, and established elaborate gardens. 711 Prince Street.

**FAWCETT HOUSE** . . . This is probably the oldest private house continuously occupied since its construction in the early 1750s, and has been the residence of the Fawcett family since 1816. The original center door was replaced by a window and the entrance changed to the side; it is otherwise as it was originally. The washroom shares the huge chimney with the kitchen fireplace. Other original dependencies are enclosed by the rear garden wall. 517 Prince Street.

**SNOWDEN HOUSE** . . . Built by Thomas Vowell, a prominent merchant, around 1800. It was purchased in 1842 by Edgar Snowden, owner of the Alexandria Gazette founded in 1784, the oldest daily newspaper in the Nation. George Washington was an early subscriber. 619 South Lee Street.

BOOTHE HOUSE . . . The rear portion dates to the mid-1700s and was built for David Griffith, the third rector of Christ Church. The front was added in 1800. Purchased by Captain William Boothe in 1853, it has remained in the family and was recently modified for office use by the law firm of Boothe, Dudley, Koontz and Blankenship. 711 Princess Street.

CAPTAINS' ROW . . . Many sea captains lived in the 100 block of Prince Street, adjacent to the waterfront; these houses are characteristic of seaport towns of Scotland and England. This block retains its cobblestone street.

THE BLUE DOOR . . . Built prior to 1779 of salmon brick covered with clapboard, the interior is preserved in its original state. The old smokehouse and spring house remain in an interesting informal garden. 708 Wolfe Street.

CORNWALL ARMS . . . It was built by Jonathon Janney shortly after 1818 and was owned by Doctor Orlando Fairfax from 1839 to 1841. The Peoples Savings and Loan Association of Alexandria has wisely adapted this fine old building for their headquarters. 301 South Washington Street.

SEAPORT INN AND DOCKSIDE SALES . . . These buildings were constructed prior to 1765 by John Patterson, "undertaker" (an eighteenth century term for contractor) and crushed oyster shells were used to mortar the twenty-eight inch stone walls. The top floor housed a large sail loft where men sewed canvas to sail the Seven Seas to bring spices and rare merchandise to the warehouses beneath, then to depart loaded with tobacco and flour. An enterprising Irish merchant, John Fitzgerald, purchased the warehouses from Patterson's widow in 1778. He was a Revolutionary officer, an aide-de-camp to General Washington, and a charter member of the Society of the Cincinnati. Today one can enjoy a gourmet meal before the Seaport Inn's ample fireplace or on the glassed balcony overlooking the Potomac. Adjacent Dockside Sales offers rare and exotic merchandise from ships that have sailed the Seven Seas. Corner of King and Union Streets at the River.

GILPIN HOUSE . . . This is an excellent example of business-residence structure, typical of early merchant-gentlemen; built in 1798 by Colonel George Gilpin. There are separate entrances for the display rooms on the first floor and the handsome living quarters in the two upper stories. The present-day Gilpin Antique Shop specializing in Colonial furnishings follows the original plan of usage. A similar building next door, The Market Square Shop, stocks fascinating decorator items and carries on the early tradition of its first owner, Bernard Chequire. 206 & 208 King Street.

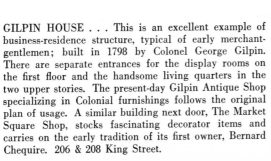

BATTERY RODGERS . . . This was one of the fortifications in the line of defense for the protection of the city of Washington during the Civil War. The site is in the 700 block of South Lee Street.

FORT WARD . . . The City of Alexandria has accurately restored the northwest bastion of Fort Ward, which was one of the largest of the sixty-eight forts and batteries which guarded the Nation's Capital. The City also erected, in a new forty acre park, a handsome museum which houses a splendid display of Civil War items, also an Officers' Hut. Both buildings were reproduced from wartime photographs. 4301 West Braddock Road.

PROVOST MARSHAL'S OFFICE . . . Civil war photograph of the building, since demolished, which stood on the north side of King Street, east of Saint Asaph.

THE VIRGINIA THEOLOGICAL SEMINARY . . . Following the Revolutionary War and the separation of Church and State, the Episcopal Church suffered a decline because of being cut off from England. A small group of men, including Francis Scott Key, dedicated to recruiting and training a new generation of Church leaders, formed an "Education Society in 1818 and five years later opened the "School of Prophets", later the Protestant Episcopal Seminary in Virginia. The first instructor there was Reuel Keith, who performed the Custis-Lee wedding ceremony, and the first two buildings were "Oakwood", which was sold to the school by Jonah Thompson and his wife in 1827, and "Melrose", the home of Dr. Edward Lippitt, professor of Systematic Divinity. Except for the Civil War period, during which it was used for a hospital by Federal troops, the Seminary has continued expansion.

GEORGE WASHINGTON MASONIC NATIONAL MEMORIAL . . . Financed by Masons throughout the Nation and its possessions, this building houses memorabilia of the Alexandria-Washington Lodge of which George Washington was the Charter Master.

SHUTER'S HILL . . . The pencil sketch shows Federal troops digging entrenchments after the defeat at Manassas. Previously, this was the site of the fine home of Ludwell Lee, son of Richard Henry Lee, a signer of the Declaration of Independence. In 1793 Ludwell Lee purchased Shuter's Hill, which is now the site of the Masonic Memorial, and was once under consideration as a site for the United States Capitol. In 1799, he conveyed this estate to Benjamin Dulany of Alexandria, and erected the elegant home, Belmont, near Leesburg, where he died in 1836.

WARWICK . . . Home of Frank Hume (1843-1905), civic and educational leader and philanthropist. He volunteered at sixteen in the Mississippi Zouaves, took part in most of the major battles of the Civil War, and was wounded at Gettysburg. In 1879 he purchased the six hundred acre estate in the suburbs of Alexandria, which he named Warwick after his family's ancestral castle in England. It burned in 1921, and in the foundation ruins was found a stone on which was chiselled, "Peach Orchard, G. W.", thought to have been a survey marker of George Washington's. The house was rebuilt, but destroyed in the 1950's for the Warwick Village Housing development. The cannon in the picture, later given to the Arlington County Court House, had been used at the White House by Andrew Jackson to fire salutes upon important occasions.

CAMERON . . . Pen and ink drawing from memory done by Major Samuel Cooper, son of General Samuel Cooper, following the Civil War. The property had been acquired in 1839 from the estate of Charles Bennett. Because General Cooper, who served his country from 1815 to 1861 in the United States Army, served with the Conferedate Army during the Civil War, his property was confiscated in 1864 and sold to the William Silverys. The Silverys conveyed it back to Mrs. Cooper who was George Mason's granddaughter. During the War, Union troops tore down the large mansion and used the bricks to build a powder magazine, still standing, in the place where the home had stood, so that when the family returned in 1865, they lived in the house in the left foreground which had been slave quarters.

COL. S COOPER'S RESIDENCE
CAMERON
1861

SUMMER HILL . . . The site of this home, which was destroyed in the 1950s for a shopping center, is on the elevation at Duke Street Extended and Longview Drive. Summer Hill was the home of Antoine Charles Cazenove, who had emigrated from Geneva, Switzerland to Philadelphia in 1795. Two years later he married and settled in Alexandria on this estate.

CLARENS . . . This was the home, erected about 1783, of Cecilia Lee, daughter of Ludwell Lee of Shuter's Hill, who married James McKenna of Alexandria. By 1839, it had become a school for boys and later became a girls' seminary. 318 North Quaker Lane.

SEMINARY HILL

MUCKROSS . . . Built in the 1830's by the Herbert family and named for the Irish abbey built in 1440 on an island in Lake Killarney, near the area from which the Herberts came. Due to its position commanding the Little River Turnpike and the railroad, Muckross was seized by Federal forces early in the Civil War and Fort Worth was constructed on the grounds, the house used by the staff officers. The five-pointed, star-shaped fort with two powder magazines, deep inner and shallow outer fortifications are well preserved. Colonel Arthur Herbert of the Confederacy regained possession and lived there until his death in 1923. St. Stephens Road.

# Arlington Heritage

MOST Arlingtonians are surprised to learn that until 1920, their community was known as Alexandria County. Its name was changed to Arlington at that date to avoid confusion with the adjacent city of the same name. Alexandria County came into being as part of the original District of Columbia and then included the town of Alexandria. In 1791, "Jurisdiction Stones" were placed at one mile intervals to mark the survey which was ordered by George Washington. The area remained a part of the District of Columbia until 1846, when it was retroceded to Virginia.

Although Arlington is the third smallest county in the nation, with only twenty-five and a half square miles, it possesses symbols of every important event in American history. In 1608, Captain John Smith wrote of the Necostin Indians on its shores. He visited the village of Nameroughquena, at the site of the Rochambeau and George Mason Memorial "Twin Bridges" and described the Indians fishing for giant sturgeon at the site of Chain Bridge.

Following Smith's visit, the area was much frequented by men engaged in the Indian fur trade, but it did not become a settled community until about 1700. The first settlers were predominantly Virginians from the lower Potomac. Early settlers were given some protection from Indian raids by the Potomac Rangers. The 1692 journal of a Ranger is preserved and describes expeditions which traversed this area on a route probably used from about 1680. It followed the old Indian and buffalo trails. By 1679, the Indians had left Arlington, moving westward.

Braddock and his men passed through Arlington in 1755, enroute to the French and Indian Wars. George Washington's diary frequently mentioned surveying his lands with his friends, Dr. David Stuart of Abingdon and the Balls of what is now Glencarlyn. The Madisons, fleeing the British invasion of Washington in 1814, crossed through Arlington enroute to the homes of their friends at Rokeby and Salona in nearby Fairfax County. Robert E. Lee is Arlington County's link with the Mexican War, in which he was breveted three times for outstanding courage and performance of duty.

The tragic events of the Civil War were a time of trial for all the good people of Arlington County. In time, twenty-two forts were erected within the county's present boundaries, as part of the defenses of Washington. The civil population was greatly outnumbered by the permanent garrison of these defenses. A proper number of local sons slipped away to don Confederate gray. A notable number of the local daughters married boys in blue, who held a monopoly of the field for four long years. And a number of those who first came to this County with weapons in their hands returned later to make their homes here.

Memorials along the Potomac and in Arlington National Cemetery honor the valor of our nation's heroes throughout its history. Arlington Memorial Bridge spans the Potomac on the axis connecting the national memorials to Abraham Lincoln and to Robert E. Lee. It symbolizes the present bond between the North and the South.

Another memorial dedicated in honor of Robert E. Lee is the Lee Highway, which now starts in Arlington County at the Virginia end of the Francis Scott Key Memorial Bridge, and continues as such to the Tennessee line at Bristol, via Routes 211 to Newmarket, thence on Route 11. However, when it was officially dedicated in June, 1923, with the President of the United States officiating, it extended from Zero Milestone back of the White House, to the Pacific Milestone in San Diego, with ceremonies at both places attended by thousands of people. Since that time, various segments of the transcontinental highway have been given other names, apparently in ignorance of the original official name!

The beautiful gateways of the Arlington National Cemetery are dedicated to outstanding officers of the Union Forces in the Civil War. The remains of four hundred Confederate soldiers were buried beneath an inspiring monument erected in 1914 by the United Daughters of the Confederacy. The inscription reads, "Not for Fame or Reward, Not for Place or for Rank, Not Lured by Ambition or Goaded by Necessity, but in Simple Obedience to Duty as They Understood it, These Men Suffered All, Sacrificed All, Dared All and Died."

Soldiers of the Spanish-American War are honored by a slender shaft topped by a spread-eagle on a globe, erected by the National Society, Colonial Dames of America. Another unusual monument is to the "Roughriders". The Navy and Marine Corps are honored by the "Battleship Maine Monument".

Another monument of great beauty is the Canadian Cross, "Erected by the Citizens of Canada in Honor of the Citizens of the United States who Served in the Canadian Army and Gave Their Lives 1914-1918."

May 30, 1958, climaxed a week dedicated by our nation to all unidentified heroes of World War II and Korea, with the interment at Arlington National Cemetery of two symbolic bodies. They rest beside the remains of the "Unknown Soldier" of World War I, before the Memorial Amphitheatre which was dedicated in May, 1920.

Arlington County is delightfully situated in a great curve of the Potomac at the "fall line" where the piedmont escarpment crosses the river, forming two-hundred foot palisades along the upper shoreline, terminating the tidal flow at Little Falls on the county line. People assigned to the National Capital from all parts of the nation and the world have been attracted by the sylvan beauty of Arlington and have sought homes here.

In 1900, this was still essentially a rural County, but thereafter it became increasingly suburban as homes and villages multiplied along the trolley lines that facilitated commuting to Washington. Now the County is almost solidly built up, except for the preservation of the lovely stream-valleys as parks. It maintained the national population growth record from 1930 to 1950, first doubling and then tripling its population.

In Arlington County, one can find true wilderness areas within three miles of the White House, and because of its elevation, a more delightful climate than in any part of the metropolitan area, yet convenient to all the cultural advantages of the Nation's Capital.

ARLINGTON HOUSE . . . Arlington's present name is derived from that of the mansion which George Washington Parke Custis built soon after 1800 on the heights overlooking the new city of Washington. He was Martha Washington's grandson, adopted by George Washington and brought up at Mount Vernon.

Mr. and Mrs. Custis had a strong feeling of responsibility for their negro servants. To some, Mr. Custis deeded homesites, and to all, he provided in his will for them to receive freedom. Mrs. Custis taught them to read and write, and where possible, provided for their training in a trade or skill which would enable them to earn a living, in order that they might be properly prepared to receive their freedom, with proper status.

The Custis' daughter married Robert Edward Lee, who came to regard Arlington House as his home, a tie which bound his allegiance to Virginia when the moment of decision came to him. He referred to Arlington as ". . . where my affections and attachments are more firmly placed than at any place in the world."

The estate was lost to the family through confiscation for taxes during the Civil War. Mrs. Lee, to whom her father had willed it in trust for his namesake grandson, was at that time a semi-invalid refugeeing in Richmond. She sent the $92.07 tax money to a cousin in Alexandria who presented it to the tax collector, who refused to accept it from the hands of any but the legal owner. The Federal Courts later termed the confiscation illegal and awarded compensation to Custis Lee.

Recognition of the qualities of greatness which Robert E. Lee possessed inspired Representative Cramton of Michigan to introduce a bill in 1925 which provided for the restoration of Arlington House in his honor. In 1955 it was, by an Act of Congress, officially designated as his permanent national memorial. Having for some years been erroneously called "The Lee Mansion", and later, "The Custis-Lee Mansion", its authentic original historical name, used and loved by the Custis and Lee family, is being officially restored to "Arlington House, the Robert E. Lee Memorial."

**MEMORIAL TO THE MEN OF THE SEA . . .**
On Columbia Island, between Arlington Memorial Bridge and the George Mason Memorial Bridge (south-bound U. S. 1) is a beautiful and unusual piece of sculpture which depicts seven sea gulls in flight above the crest of a billowing wave. It is the work of Beni del Piatta. The inscription reads, "To Strong Souls and Ready Valor of Those Men of the United States Who in the Navy, the Merchant Marine, and Other Paths of Activity Upon the Waters of the World Have Given Life or Still Offer It in the Performance of Heroic Deeds, This Monument is Dedicated by a Grateful People."

**TOMB OF THE UNKNOWNS . . .** "Here rest in honored glory an American soldier known but to God." May 30, 1958 climaxed a week dedicated to the honor of all unidentified heroes of World War II and Korea, with the interment at Arlington National Cemetery of two symbolic bodies. They rest beside the remains of the "Unknown Soldier" of World War I, before the Memorial Amphitheatre which was dedicated in May, 1920.

THE MAST OF THE MAINE . . . Beneath the actual mast of the Battleship Maine, blown up in Havana Harbor, 1898, lie the remains of two hundred and thirty-one American servicemen who lost their lives in the disaster. In a vault beneath the mast also lies the body of Ignace Jan Paderewski, one of the world's greatest pianists and statesmen, a former Premier and President of Poland. Before his death in this country in 1941, he had requested that his heart be removed before burial and given into the custody of loyal American citizens of Polish descent and that his remains lie on American soil until Poland should become free. It was his wish that eventually his heart might be placed in Warsaw Cathedral near that of Frederic Chopin. A quarter of a century later, the vaults bears no inscription, awaiting fulfillment of his wish.

THE JOHN FITZGERALD KENNEDY MEMORIAL . . . In the spring of 1963, President Kennedy and Secretary Robert McNamara, seeking a moment of relief from the cares of office in these troubled times, went privately to Arlington House. There, in the room in which Robert E. Lee, in agony of spirit, had written his resignation from the United States Army, they paid homage to his strength and nobility of character. Afterwards, on the lawn in front of the house, the President, enjoying the beauty of the spring day and the view of Washington, was moved to exclaim, "I could stay here forever!" . . . In November, he was laid to rest at the foot of Arlington House lawn.

THE NETHERLANDS CARILLON . . . The bells, cast in Holland, were donated by the people of The Netherlands as a token of gratitude for liberation from the Nazis and for American post-war aid. The official presentation was made in Washington at Meridian Hill Park by Queen Juliana during her visit in 1952. The permanent installation was made just north of Arlington National Cemetery in 1959 and is the site of the area's Easter Sunrise Service. The tower was designed by Joost W. C. Boks and the bronze lions by Paul Koning.

MEMORIAL TO THE UNITED STATES MARINES . . . This gigantic statue (seventy-eight feet high including the base) of five Marines and one Sailor raising the American flag on Mount Suribachi, Iwo Jima Island, is in a small park north of Arlington National Cemetery. It is the work of sculptor Felix W. deWeldon who was on duty with the Navy when the photograph by Joe Rosenthal was transmitted to headquarters. Mr. deWeldon was so inspired that he worked uninterruptedly forty-eight hours to complete a small scale model. From this, he made a life-size model which is placed at the entrance to the Quantico Marine Base. His engineering marvel is the statue in Arlington. On the base is inscribed, "Uncommon Valor was a Common Virtue."

ARTILLERY, FT. MYER . . . White Horse Battery racing across the parade ground. Fort Myer became a permanent cavalry post in 1902 on a site which had been a military installation since the Civil War. The cavalry was mechanized during World War II, but twenty-eight horses remain for state affairs and military funerals. Since World War II, Fort Myer has been the headquarters of the First Battle Group, Third Infantry, the Nation's oldest active Regular Army Infantry unit, known as "The Old Guard". The towers in the background were the world's foremost radio station, installed by the Navy in 1913 and removed in 1941. Located on Arlington Boulevard adjacent to Arlington National Cemetery.

THE PENTAGON . . . This five-sided colossus, built in 1941-43, and having seventeen and a half miles of corridors, is the largest office building in the world. Located near the convergence of Shirley Memorial and Jefferson Davis Highways near the Potomac.

SPOUT RUN PARKWAY
. . . As it converges with the George Washington Memorial Parkway.

RIVER SCENE . . . Typical of the tranquil beauty to be found along the shores of the Potomac.

ABINGDON . . . Built prior to 1741 by members of the Alexander family, the home was destroyed by fire in 1930. John Alexander emigrated from Scotland in 1659 and ten years later purchased six thousand acres, for six hogsheads of tobacco, extending in a two-mile wide strip from Hunting Creek south of Alexandria to north of Arlington Cemetery. His heirs sold more than two thousand acres in 1779 to Martha Washington's son, John Parke Custis. His son, George Washington Parke Custis, built his home "Arlington House" on the northern part of his inheritance. Abingdon ruins are on the hilltop between Washington National Airport and George Washington Memorial Parkway.

WASHINGTON NATIONAL AIRPORT . . . Located in south Arlington on the site of Abingdon Plantation, the picture shows Alexandria in the background.

THE GLEBE HOUSE . . . Erected in 1775 as a rectory for the minister of the newly formed Fairfax Parish, its site was chosen midway between the two churches, Christ Church in Alexandria and The Falls Church. Partially burned in 1809, it was rebuilt in 1820 utilizing the original walls and foundations. The octagon portion was probably added by a later occupant, the noted sculptor Clark Mills among whose works are the equestrian statues of Andrew Jackson in Lafayette Park and George Washington in Washington Circle in the Federal City. Among other notable residents were Mayor Peter Van Ness of Washington who married Marcia Burns, whose father's farm had been sold for the site of the White House. The Glebe House was later the home of Count Caleb Cushing, our first minister to China. In order to negotiate with the Emperor who gave audience only to nobility a title was conferred upon him in 1844 by the President of the United States; an unconstitutional act of expediency. 4527 Seventeenth Street, North.

SPLENDOR THAT HAS VANISHED . . . First called Ruthcomb and renamed Altha Hall by later owners, this Greek Revival mansion was built in 1889 by Andrew Adgate Lipscomb, II of Fairfax, who became Assistant District Attorney of the District of Columbia. This was the scene of much social life. Remnants of Fort Strong form part of the landscaping of the garden. Both the fort and the mansion were destroyed in 1959 and replaced by the Potomac Towers Apartments.

GREEN VALLEY MANOR . . . Built by Anthony Fraser about 1821, this handsome residence was destroyed by fire in 1924. The estate was acquired by the Fraser family in the mid-1700's and was the scene of considerable activity during the Civil War, including the establishment of an early convalescent camp. Across Shirley Highway from the homesite is the family cemetery, on the grounds of the Army-Navy Country Club.

— 58 —

RIXEY MANSION . . . Picture taken at the time it was purchased for Marymount Junior College, it is now the center building of a vast educational complex. A pre-Civil War farmhouse was purchased about 1902 by Admiral Presley M. Rixey who became Assistant Surgeon General of the Navy and White House Physician. The original house burned about 1920 and was replaced by this mansion where the Admiral resided until his death in 1928. North Glebe Road, south of the Washington Golf and Country Club at Yorktown Boulevard.

DOUBLEDAY MANSION . . . The oldest portion may have been built in the early 1800s, the wings were added in 1898 by Colonel Charles William Doubleday, creating a mansion which he called "The Cedars". Since the early 1900s, numerous owners have enjoyed the magnificent view down the Potomac from the crest of the Palisades. 2301 North Uhle Street.

HUME SCHOOL . . . Erected 1895, this is the oldest standing school building in the County. It was named to honor Frank Hume who gave part of the land within its grounds. The building was deeded by Arlington County to the Arlington Historical Society which in 1963 restored it for a museum and for public meetings. Open 2 to 4 each Sunday afternoon. 1801 South Arlington Ridge Road.

ARLINGTON MILL RUINS . . . This mill was erected George Washington Parke Custis on Washington Fore lands at the Columbia Pike crossing of Four Mile Ru Destroyed during the Civil War.

BIRCHWOOD . . . Erected during the 1830s by Caleb Birch, this log cabin was beautifully restored with additions in 1939. 4572 Twenty-sixth Street, North.

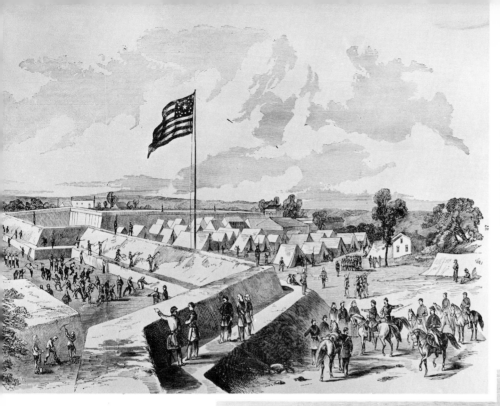

CAMP CORCORAN . . . Later termed "Fort Corcoran" (576 yards perimeter), it was constructed on the brink of the hill above Rosslyn for the protection of the Aqueduct Bridge and the road from Falls Church which is the present Wilson Boulevard.

GENERAL McDOWELL'S ADVANCE TO FAIRFAX COURTHOUSE . . . To the right foreground is the present road to McLean, Route 123. The troops are shown crossing the old Pimmit Run Bridge, the stone abutment of which can be seen today a few yards above the existing bridge. They are moving up Chain Bridge Hill, little changed in the past century.

CAMP MARCY, V.ª near Chain Bridge, 132ⁿᵈ Regᵗ. N.Y.S.Volˢ
Col. Leonard Bayer, Comm'dᵍ

CAMP MARCY . . . Just over the line in Fairfax County, this camp soon became Fort Marcy, which flanked the twenty-two fortifications which were placed in Arlington County as part of the Defenses of Washington. It is preserved by the National Park Service with an entrance from the north-bound lane of the George Washington Memorial Parkway.

# Fairfax Heritage

ATTEMPTS were made and failed four times in the Assembly before Fairfax County, named after Thomas, sixth Lord Fairfax, Baron of Cameron, was created from the northern portion of Prince William County in 1742. The area had first been established as Truro Parish, named after a shipping port in Cornwall, England, known for the tin and copper ore found in its vicinity. Early explorers thought that they had found copper deposits around Frying Pan and Horsepen Runs.

On the same day the act creating the County was approved, the Council directed that the courthouse be built at a place called "Spring Field" situated between the New Church Road (now Route 7) and the Ox Road (Route 123, near Floris) "in the branches of Difficult Run, Hunting Creek and Accotinck". The particular site selected was on the main highway of that day, the New Church or Ridge Road which ran from Hunting Creek on the Potomac River past The Falls Church to Key's Gap in the Blue Ridge Mountains. Six acres of land at what is now called Freedom Hill were given by William Fairfax, limiting the gift to the time the court was held there and no longer.

William Fairfax of Belvoir was a Burgess, the first county lieutenant and presiding justice in the county court. Lewis Elzey was the first sheriff.

The site of the first courthouse was marked by a stone and bronze plaque some years ago by the Fairfax Chapter of the Daughters of the American Revolution and is located on the west side of Route 123, one half mile south of Tyson's Corner. The marker reads: "From this spot N. 20° W. 220′, stood the first Court House of Fairfax County, built in 1742, abandoned because of Indian Hostilities about 1752." The stone has recently been moved a few feet from its original position on the roadside because of highway development.

Documentation is lacking to verify the Indian menace and it is more likely that the business interests and the offer of a courthouse building in Alexandria prevailed. This second courthouse was located on the east side of Market Square facing Fairfax Street between Cameron and King Streets, opposite the Carlyle House.

Catesby Cocke, the first clerk of Fairfax County, was the son of Dr. William Cocke, the Secretary of the Colony, 1712-1720, and had himself already served as Clerk of Stafford County, 1729-1731, and Prince William County, 1731-1742.

The first settlements of the county were, of course, along the Potomac and its tributaries—Colchester on Belmont Bay was a planned community authorized by the Virginia Assembly in 1753. Laid out on paper before settlement, it was located on the lands of Peter Wagener. John West's survey of 1754 shows a triangular town of forty-one lots and a market square. The town enjoyed a short prosperity but like Dumfries and Occoquan was doomed when silt filled up the shipping channel. A tragic fire eventually wiped out the entire village except for two buildings which are still standing, one of them being the Fairfax Arms, the other too modified to bear any resemblance to its original form. Further up the Potomac, the Masons and Washingtons were developing their lands.

The second George Mason established himself at Pohick Creek on the Potomac River in the 1690's and his son, George Mason III lived there until about 1730, at which time he moved across the River to Charles County, Maryland. As late as 1722, the Mason's house at Pohick was named in Governor Spotswood's treaty with the Iroquois as the frontier location to which to deliver runaway slaves.

In the Truro vestry book, the parish church was referred to as "Occoquan Church" until 1733, at which time the name "Pohick" was assumed, indicating that the building was near the ford where the Potomac Path crossed Pohick Run. Bishop Meade wrote as follows:

"The Old Pohick Church was a frame building and occupied a site on the south side of Pohick Run, and about two miles from the present, which is on the north side of the run. When it was no longer fit for use, it is said the parishioners were called together to determine on the locality of the new church, when George Mason, the compatriot of Washington, and senior vestryman, advocated the old site, pleading that it was the house in which their fathers worshiped, and that the graves of many were around it, while Washington and others advocated a more central and convenient one . . . Washington surveyed the neighborhood, and marked the houses and distances on a well-drawn map, and when the day of decision arrived, met all the arguments of his opponent by presenting this paper, and thus carried his point."

Captain Augustine Washington moved his family including young George, who was then three years old, from Wakefield to the Little Hunting Creek Plantation in 1735. The modest home burned in 1739, and the family then moved to Ferry Farm on the Rappahannock opposite Fredericksburg.

George Washington's half-brother, Lawrence, came of age in 1740 and also into possession of the northern plantation. He married Anne Fairfax of Belvoir. He commanded a colonial army unit in an amphibious attack on Cartagena commanded by Admiral Vernon, and named the estate in his honor. George came to live with his brother and sister-in-law while in his teens and began his career as a surveyor. Lawrence died in 1752 and willed Mount Vernon to George who later bought out his widowed sister-in-law's life interest. He married Martha Dandridge Custis, a young widow with two children, John and "Patsy", who grew up at Mount Vernon. John married and had four children. When he died, the Washingtons adopted the two younger ones, Eleanor Parke Custis (called Nelly, who became the mistress of "Woodlawn") and George Washington Parke Custis (called Parke, who became the master of "Arlington House").

By the time the county had become a separate entity, Robert Carter had patented thousands of acres of land in the area in anticipation of a lucrative copper mining operation. He had attempted without success to gain access to the Potomac River below Little Falls, so he built a road from the north side of Occoquan Creek to his Frying Pan mines in the vicinity of Floris. The road followed the route of an old Indian trail and is still in use as Route 123 to Fairfax City, then by Route 50 to Pender. Cornish miners were brought in for the mining operation, but the rumor of copper ore proved false. However, the influence of this venture is still felt because this road and Walter Griffin's Rolling Road (the Colchester Road), were for many years the only roads connecting the Potomac area with the Piedmont and the Shenandoah Valley.

The second important road, built in 1750, went from Alexandria to Newgate (now Centreville) and turned west to join the Ox Road (Route 123). It was named Braddock Road, in the hope which George Washington shared with many local residents, that Braddock would use it on his march to Fort Duquesne, thereby further clearing it through the forests. Instead, part of Braddock's troops used the Ridge Road past Falls Church to Leesburg, and part took a route through Maryland.

Before 1790, the Fauquier and Alexandria Road was built and along it the towns of Providence, Centreville, Haymarket, Buckland, and Warrenton eventually came into being.

Roads were a problem in Virginia in general and in Fairfax County in particular. There are many accounts of travelers all through the 1700's wherein they became completely lost on a main road or hopelessly mired in the red clay which was excellent for brickmaking but terrible for vehicles and horses.

When Pennsylvania organized a stock company and built a tollroad in the 1790's, both Alexandria and Georgetown adopted the idea as a means of improving the routes to the Shenandoah Valley. The most important was the Little River Turnpike, now Route 236 from Alexandria to Fairfax City, then Route 50 to Winchester. As late as 1838, Congress authorized a public lottery to raise money to improve the Middle Turnpike from Alexandria to "Drane's Tavern" at Dranesville in order to justify charging tolls for the use of the road.

After the Revolution, the dilapidated condition of the courthouse and the threat of the absorption of Alexandria into the new Federal District made another move of the county seat necessary. After ten years of discussions and proposals, the Assembly directed the Fairfax Court to select a central location, considering their simultaneous redrawing of the Loudoun-Fairfax boundary line, this time at Sugarland Run. This change of boundary explains why records of land transfers and other transactions which took place between 1757 and 1797, north of Centreville, Difficult Run and Great Falls are found in the Loudoun County Courthouse.

Work on the third courthouse was begun in 1799. The site selected was the crossing of the Little River Turnpike (Route 236) and the Ox Road (Route 123), on two acres of land deeded by Richard Ratcliffe. It was constructed of brick and in use by the time George Washington's will was probated and recorded there on January 20, 1800 by George Deneale, County Clerk. In 1805 an Act of the Assembly established a town by the name of Providence at Fairfax Court House. The name of the county seat was changed to Town of Fairfax in 1874, and to the City of Fairfax in 1961. (The

newer additions to the court house building have been harmonious with the old architecture, and the original building has been recently restored by the county.)

The Patowmack Canal Company was chartered in 1784 in an effort to connect the waters of the Ohio with the rivers in Virginia. The construction of the locks at Great Falls for the navigation system was an engineering marvel of the day. But there were only an average of forty-five days each year when the river was high enough to permit navigation over some of the shallow places, so the company conveyed its works and franchises to the Chesapeake and Ohio Canal Company in 1828 for the construction of a slack water canal on the Maryland side. However, the Baltimore and Ohio Railroad won the construction race to the Ohio River and thus began a new era in the history of commerce.

The largest tavern in Northern Virginia in Washington's day was the Eagle Tavern in Newgate, or Centreville, as it was named in 1792. Washington stayed at the hostelry numerous times. The building, which fell down in the 1930's, was located on Braddock Road close to its intersection with Lee Highway. On the upper floor was one large bedroom for men, another for women, and each of the beds slept five people. An amusing story was written in a letter by a traveler who stayed there one night. He stood it as long as he could, but about four in the morning he finally woke the man who was sleeping next to him and asked him to please remove his spurs.

The Civil War is to some extent covered in the captions of the pictures which follow. Fairfax County was very heavily involved in the War, troops of both sides constantly marching back and forth. Centreville was the area where over 40,000 troops were encamped for a winter during which the generals kept the soldiers busy by having them build earthworks up to twenty feet high and six miles long. The details of the period from 1861 to 1865 have been given in many books written on the subject, and there is not sufficient space here to do it justice.

As one of the fastest growing counties in the nation, Fairfax County is now prosperous with a bright future. The new Northern Virginia Community College, and the George Mason Branch of the University of Virginia are both located near the City of Fairfax. The largest Army Engineering Post of the Nation is Fort Belvoir, on the site of the original Fairfax family manor house.

The George Washington Memorial Parkway extends up the Potomac Palisades as far as Cabin John Bridge, where it converges with the Capital Beltway which sweeps through Fairfax County in a crescent to the lower crossing of the Potomac on the Woodrow Wilson Memorial Bridge at Alexandria. Resembling an arrow shot from the bow of this highway is the new Route 66 leading to Prince William and Fauquier Counties.

HICKORY HILL . . . Constructed on the foundations of a much earlier house which was burned during the Civil War. It has been the home of Associate Supreme Court Justice Robert Jackson and the late John F. Kennedy when he was a Senator. On a hearthstone is a bronze plaque which reads, "N.O.N. Historical Marker —On This Spot, February 29, 1776, Absolutely Nothing Happened."

MERRYWOOD . . . Built about 1905 on the Potomac Palisades, this was the residence of Mr. and Mrs. Hugh Auchincloss and the girlhood home of Jacqueline Bouvier who married John F. Kennedy. The estate was involved in a proposal by the United States Department of the Interior to preserve scenic easements along the Potomac.

LITTLE FALLS . . . Located on the Palisades just above this historic cataract, this Regency home is curved to allow every room to have a view of the Potomac River.

McLEAN COMMUNITY

CHARMED CIRCLE . . . The sunken garden, designed by landscape architect Lester Collins, has posts garlanded with smilax, festooned with ropes and topped with stylized peacocks.

MERRYHILL . . . Formerly "Chestnut Hill," this home was built after the Civil War by John Madison Shafer on old foundations of a house which had been burned. Mrs. Shafer was famous for her "sun cooked strawberry preserves", which she prepared on the upstairs porch. The family took in drovers for overnight, who were bound for the city markets.

SALONA . . . the home of a Presbyterian minister from South Carolina, William Maffitt, who about 1800 married Henrietta Lee. The Maffitts were friends of the Madisons, and when the British entered Washington in August 1814, James Madison refugeed at Salona, where Dolley planned to meet him. However, as she was delayed and evening came on, she stopped about a mile away at Rokeby with her friend Mrs. Richard Love (neé Matilda Lee of Shuter's Hill, Alexandria), going on to Salona the next morning. Rokeby burned before the Civil War, and its Madison story has erroneously been transferred to a handsome home by that name near Leesburg.

ST. JOHN'S CHURCH . . . This building was completed in 1878, after much discussion and the rejection of the offer of a lot directly across the street from the old tavern. One faction said that proximity to a barroom or, as one designated it, "the very gates of hell", was no place for a church, whereas the other faction held that such was an ideal place for it. In 1908, when the Vestry decided to move the building closer to the trolley line, the building was placed on giant casters and rolled across two miles of sodded fields to its new location.

COLONEL EGLIN HOUSE . . . Possibly residence of overseer of "Woodberry," the 1724 grant to George Turberville of Westmoreland County. Remained in family possession through the 1700's, thence to the Hunter family. Inherited by Colonel H. W. T. Eglin, first President of the Historical Society of Fairfax County, who added portico and several rooms in the 1940's.

BIENVENUE . . . Possibly this was the smaller stone house erected by Commodore Thomas ap Catesby Jones, which was enlarged in 1859 (then spelled Benvenue) by his estate executors in accordance with his will, to provide a good residence for his Negro servants. It was used as a hospital by Federal troops during the Civil War. Sharon, the manor house, was destroyed 1960 by a subdivision developer.

EVANS FARM INN . . . where one may dine on colonial plantation food in a charming inn reconstructed from materials salvaged from old mills, inns, churches, and barns which were being demolished for highways and shopping centers. The home of the proprietors nearby was actually an early tavern which was built in 1886 by the Besley family, French Huguenots, two members of which were killed while serving with the Continental Army in the Revolution.

MAPLEWOOD . . . Built in 1870 by John Shipman and originally called "Villa Nova". Outstanding example of Second Empire style. Destroyed 1970.

JACKSON HOUSE . . . This was the home of James Jackson, owner of the Union Hotel at Fairfax Courthouse. In 1860 he became the proprietor of the Marshall House in Alexandria. On May 24, 1861, when the Union Army invaded Virginia, he shot and killed young Colonel Ephraim Elmer Ellsworth who had just removed Jackson's Confederate flag from the hotel flagpole. Jackson, in turn, was killed by Ellsworth's sergeant.

TOMBSTONE . . . Of James Jackson in the family burying ground at McLean.

DOWER HOUSE . . . A harmonious combination of old and new in architecture and furnishings distinguishes this country house. The central portion was a one-room log cabin, a widow's dower of the Jackson family of pioneer times. Seasoned materials were used for recent additions. Adam, Chippendale, Victorian, Regency and Oriental styles and designs coexist happily here.

PEACOCK HOUSE . . . This property was mentioned in George Washington's will as follows, "This tract for the size of it is valuable; more for its situation than for its soil though that is good for farming . . . It lyes on the Great Road from the City of Washington, Alexandria and George Town to Leesburg and Winchester at Difficult Bridge . . ." Washington's executors sold the property to the Sheppards of Fairfax and it was later purchased by Thomas Peacock, during whose ownership the house was a station on the Great Falls Railway.

MADEIRA SCHOOL . . . Founded in 1906 by Lucy Madeira Wing, this school for girls was moved in 1931 from Washington to its present one hundred and sixty acre campus. It includes the largest natural growth of botanical specimens in the Washington area, besides magnificent cliffs, stream valleys, natural ponds and river vistas. The school's philosophy is expressed by three traditional ideals; belief in the dignity of the individual and one's responsibility to the community; a conviction that one is morally bound to give one's best to every undertaking; and a realization that man is most productive in a climate of freedom of intellect and spirit.

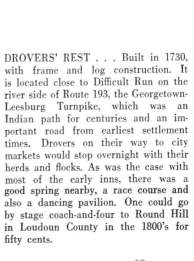

DROVERS' REST . . . Built in 1730, with frame and log construction. It is located close to Difficult Run on the river side of Route 193, the Georgetown-Leesburg Turnpike, which was an Indian path for centuries and an important road from earliest settlement times. Drovers on their way to city markets would stop overnight with their herds and flocks. As was the case with most of the early inns, there was a good spring nearby, a race course and also a dancing pavilion. One could go by stage coach-and-four to Round Hill in Loudoun County in the 1800's for fifty cents.

— 69 —

SPRING HILL . . . Built in 1780, this was the home of one Swink, who operated a mill nearby. During the Civil War, Mosby is said to have hidden in the attic.

BLACK OAK . . . In the yard of Spring Hill stands this majestic tree, largest black oak in Virginia, and fifth largest in the United States.

DIFFICULT RUN PARK . . . Once owned by the Potomac Electric Power Company, this National Park is a primitive, beautiful area named for the wild stream on the park boundary. It tumbles over jagged boulders on its way to the Potomac River.

TOWLSTON GRANGE . . . This charming house, built between 1775 and 1780 stands on the "House Lot" once owned by Bryan, eighth Lord Fairfax, at whose home Washington often visited. The present owners did major restoration and built additions when they purchased the place in 1932.

## GREAT FALLS COMMUNITY

FOUR STAIRS . . . Takes its name from the four different staircases in the house. The handsomest is inside the front door, with balusters of cherry and a walnut hand rail. The entire staircase was brought from England by the Jackson family, to whom George II was said to have granted 3,000 acres in 1740. The house was built in three sections: 1740, 1840 and 1940.

HITAFFER ROAD . . . This charming county home is located off Towlston Road. When extensive repairs and additions were made in 1940, the house was estimated to be two hundred years old, because of the methods of construction including the use of old logs covered with weatherboarding. It overlooks a forest glade along Rocky Run.

CORNWELL FARM . . .
Also known as "Fairview",
was probably built in the
early 1800's and is similar
in design to the spacious
mansions of Virginia planters along the James River.
It is on land which was
once part of the Great
Falls Manor of Thomas
Sixth Lord Fairfax.

HIDDEN SPRINGS
FARM . . . A winding
driveway off River Bend
Road near Great Falls
leads to this attractive
house, built in several different periods. The pres-
ent owner was delighted to
find beautiful pine under
many coats of paint. The
original hardware remains
on some of the extra-wide
doors. The wooden mantles
are carved and dadoed in
painstaking detail. The
roof of the large veranda is
supported by rough-hewn
log beams from an ancient
log cabin which was for-
merly part of the house.

GUNNELL'S RUN . . . The log and frame dwelling built in the early 1700's was originally owned by William Gunnell. It has had a number of additions, including one in the 1930's which was a wedding gift to Rixey Smith, the owner at that time. Several of his friends bought an old tavern in Fredericksburg and had it moved to the site and attached to the house, where it is now used as a dining room. The gravestones of Nancy and William Gunnell, which were lying in the yard, were salvaged and incorporated into one of the chimneys when restoration work was done.

TEMPLE SMITH HOUSE . . . Possibly built about 1739 on part of a tract of land patented by Thomas Lewis in 1725. In 1836 his heirs sold the property to James Oliver, whose grandson, Temple Smith, inherited it. State Senator Walter T. Oliver is buried in the family cemetery. An interesting recluse known as "Dirty Davis" once lived here. Several additions have been made to the house, including a recent one by architect Bradford de Wolf. Though the house is of substantial size now, it retains its rustic cabin appearance from the roadway.

QUIET POOL ALONG
THE VIRGINIA SHORE . . .

PICNIC AREA . . . On the Palisades
above the Falls, with a magnificent view,
is a shady grove for relaxing, with a merry-
go-round for the youngsters. For years
two different carousels were in use which
had all kinds of animals carefully carved
in wood. There used to be a large and
friendly blacksnake who lived under the
carousel, and he loved to crawl from his
secret home and lie on the central mecha-
nism to enjoy the music.

GREAT FALLS
OF THE POTOMAC

OLD FISH LADDER
IN THE POTOMAC
. . . A series of pools
allowed fish to migrate
upstream for spawning.

GREAT FALLS IN WINTER . . . In 1913,
the British Ambassador, Lord Bryce, re-
marked in an address on the Great Falls
Area "No European city has so noble a
cataract in its vicinity as the Great Falls
of the Potomac, a magnificent piece of
scenery which you will, of course, always
preserve."

CLIFF OF THE POTOMAC GORGE . . .

THE "POTOWMACK COMPANY" . . . chartered in 1785 with George Washington as its first president, for the purpose of establishing water transportation to the Ohio settlements by constructing a series of canal locks to by-pass Great Falls. Five years later, the town of Matildaville was granted a charter for 40 acres of Bryan Fairfax land. Among the trustees was "Light-Horse Harry" Lee (father of the Confederate General), whose first wife was a second-cousin, Matilda Lee, for whom the town was named. The town flourished with considerable traffic consisting mainly of wheat, flour and whiskey, from 1797 until 1828, when competition of land transportation became too great. Nothing remains except fragments of the stone walls of the superintendent's home, a stone marker, and portions of the canal and locks.

POTOMAC PALISADES SHOWING GEOLOGICAL STRATA . . .

CANAL BLASTED AND CUT
THROUGH SOLID CLIFF

MASONRY WALLS OF THE CANAL

STONECUTTER'S
IDENTIFICATION
MARK . . .

MATILDAVILLE RUINS . . .
Remnants of the walls of the
home of the superintendent.

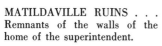

GREAT FALLS RAIL-WAY . . . Great Falls Park was a mecca for Washingtonians and people of the Northern Virginia area, who boarded the electric trolley at Rosslyn and rode up through the Virginia countryside to spend a day at the park. Abandoned in 1935 after 29 years of operation, the right-of-way is the present Old Dominion Drive.

DICKEY'S TAVERN . . . First known as Mrs. Myer's Tavern, Dickey's was a landmark for generations of visitors to Great Falls and Matildaville. It has been said that Presidents from George Washington to Theodore Roosevelt visited there. Burned June 23, 1949.

LAKE BARCROFT . . . Waters are impounded by what is probably the highest stone masonry dam in Virginia. A large flock of Canada geese call this lake home.

through the installation of storm drainage facilities and the planting of various types of vegetative materials. Many of these plants have been supplied by the Soil Conservation Service of the United States Department of Agriculture. A large flock of Canada Geese call Lake Barcroft home.

## BAILEY'S CROSSROADS AREA

BARCROFT MILL . . . Deeds dating back to the 1700's refer to this property as "Adams Mill Lot", which was acquired by Ambrose Barcroft in 1848 but it is unclear whether the old mill was still standing or a new one was built. During the Civil War the mill was heavily damaged and although Dr. John Woolverton Barcroft took title to the property in 1866, he apparently decided instead to rebuild Arlington Mill on Four Mile Run. The mill ruins are downstream from Lake Barcroft on Holmes Run.

BAILEY'S CROSSROADS . . .
With Munson's Hill in the background up the Leesburg pike.

CHURCH HILL . . . Built about 1750 by Colonel William Adams. The first Methodist preaching in the area was done here, and Bishop Francis Asbury was often a visitor. Simon Adams, who served in the Kentucky Legislature, was born here. Demolished 1965 for erection of Rochambeau Apartments. The family graves are beneath the playground of J. E. B. Stuart High School nearby.

**GREEN SPRING FARM . . .** Family and local traditions hold that John Moss built the central portion about 1760. The brick work on the front is Flemish bond, on the sides and back, English bond. Three members of the Moss family were Fairfax County Court Clerks at different times in the 1800's. Fountain Beattie, military associate and close friend of John Mosby bought the property and lived here after the Civil War. Many social, civic, religious and political notables have been entertained here through the years.

**RAVENSWORTH STABLE AND CARRIAGE HOUSE . . .** Destroyed for a housing development in the early 1960's, the mansion was erected about 1800 by William Fitzhugh, formerly of Chatham near Fredericksburg, on the 22,000 acre plantation which his emigrant great grandfather had bought from grantee John Matthews in 1685, later confirmed by direct grant in 1694. The home was destroyed by an incendiary fire in 1926. It was at Ravensworth that Mrs. Robert E. Lee and the Lee girls sought refuge when they fled from Arlington House in April, 1861, and where General Lee's mother was nursed during her last illness.

OAK HILL . . . Old records show that there were buildings on the Oak Hill and Ossian Hall portions of the original Ravensworth estate as early as 1730 and 1735 respectively, but these were probably tenant houses. It is likely that Oak Hill was built by Lund Washington in 1758, when he was employed by Major Fitzhugh to manage the portion of the estate inherited from his father. As is the case with many old homes, the portico was added in recent times.

## ANNANDALE
## AREA

OSSIAN HALL . . . deliberately burned by the Fairfax County Fire Department, September 3, 1959, after vandals had ravaged it following sale for a housing development. It was probably built in 1783 by Nicholas Fitzhugh, the first member of the family to reside on the Ravensworth estate. It was named for a popular legendary Gaelic warrior whose exploits were published in "Tamora" in 1763.

Ossian Hall was sold in 1804 to Dr. David Stuart, prominent statesman and husband of Martha Washington's widowed daughter-in-law. Married in 1783, they had resided for ten years at the Custis home, Abingdon, before moving to Hope Park in Fairfax County, where they remained until moving to Ossian Hall.

HOPE PARK . . . Built about 1750, probably by Edward Payne, builder of Payne's Church. He sold 1250 acres to Dr. David Stuart in 1785. Dr. Stuart married Eleanor Calvert Custis, the widow of Martha Washington's son. The Stuarts first resided at Abingdon and then at Hope Park before moving to Ossian Hall. George Washington's diary mentions that he and his wife dined and spent the night at Hope Park on May 17, 1798.

HOPE PARK MILLER'S HOUSE . . .

HOPE PARK MILL . . . Also known as Piney Branch Mill and Robey's Mill. Erected about 1820.

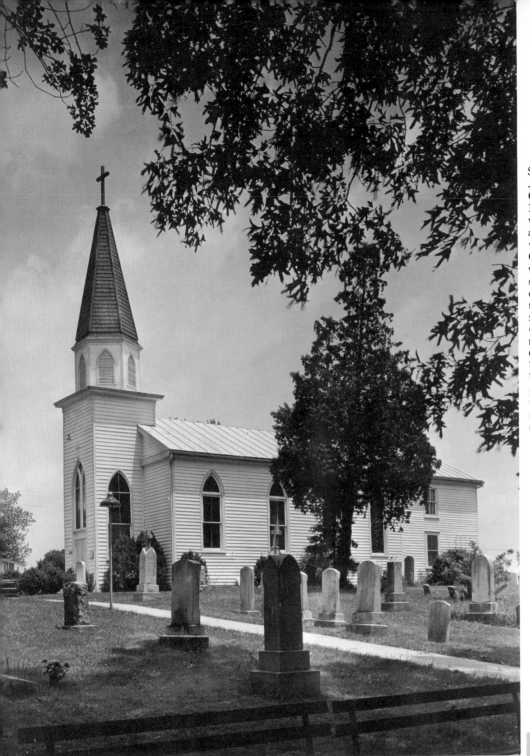

SAINT MARY'S CHURCH . . . This lovely little Roman Catholic Church was built in 1858 for the Irish immigrants who were building the Orange and Alexandria Railroad. It was close to this church that Clara Barton rendered aid to wounded soldiers, for the second time in a major battle of the Civil War. Her work throughout the war led to the founding of the American Red Cross. There is a local legend that, when General U. S. Grant became President of the United States, he learned that Union soldiers had used the pews of the church for firewood and immediately furnished new ones which are still in use.

## FAIRFAX STATION AREA

INNISFAIL . . . Erected about 1770. Once home of George Deneale, first Fairfax County Clerk after new courthouse was built in Providence (now Fairfax City) in 1800.

BRIMSTONE HILL . . . The oldest part dates back before 1810 and was originally a "house of private entertainment" (serving food to hungry travelers). It later became a "house of public entertainment" (serving both food and spirits to travelers). Civil War records referred to it as Arundel's Farm, where Confederate troops were surprised by an attack by Federal troops who had heard that the former were planning to raid some supply trains at nearby Burke Station. There was a skirmish and hard riding as the Confederates headed for Wolf Run Shoals on Occoquan Creek, where the Union troops abandoned the chase. This was the last skirmish of the **Civil War in Virginia. On the old Ox Road.**

## BURKE-FAIRFAX STATION AREA

QUAILWOOD . . . This house, gracious in its typical southern architecture, dates back in part to 1833, although the portico was added in recent years. Located on Wolf Run Shoals Road in Terrapin Hollow, trenches and earthworks remain nearby as reminders of Civil War skirmishes which took place in the area.

ROMAN ARCADES . . .
Part of the Workhouse Division of the D.C. Department of Corrections at Occoquan, Virginia (Lorton), located on a 3500 acre reservation made up of small parcels of land acquired from 1909 on. The buildings shown were begun in 1924, constructed by inmate labor of bricks made on the place.

5500 ROLLING ROAD . . . Built in 1962 on part of the old Fitzhugh estate. The land with its gently rolling conformation and the prominence of the site chosen for the house were reminiscent of the settings for the great Virginia plantation houses of the 1700's. This influenced the design toward a stately, contemporary plantation house from which views of the land could be had. The barrel vaults, an ancient device, create interior spaces from which dramatic sky views are obtained. The architect was Charles M. Goodman, and the owner is a descendant of Thomson Mason, who brought William Buckland to America to do the interior of his brother's "Gunston Hall".

MOUNT GILEAD . . . Built after 1750, this house was operated as the Black Horse Tavern by Joel Beach from 1785-1789. During the winter of 1861-1862, nearly 40,000 troops were quartered at Centreville, during which time General Joseph E. Johnston probably used Mount Gilead as his personal quarters.

MILLER'S HOUSE . . . James Cabell, an early miller, probably erected this house and the adjacent mill in the 1830's, although he did not acquire title until 1865.

WALNEY . . . The large spring house may date back to 1727, date of the land grant. Local tradition is that the stone dwelling was built by Hessian soldiers in 1789. However, extensive remodelings of the 1840's, 1870's and 1940's have obliterated evidences of early construction techniques. In 1843, the property was purchased by Lewis H. Machen who named his home for an island off the coast of Lancashire, England. An employee of the United States Senate, he became the first commuter to Washington. On Centreville Road near Rocky Run.

## CENTREVILLE AREA

THE MILL . . . Included with the Miller's House and Walney in the ELLANOR C. LAWRENCE COUNTY PARK of 640 acres, presented to Fairfax County in 1970 by publisher David Lawrence as a memorial to his late wife. This estate is part of the original grant of 1727 to Major George Turberville, which he called "Golden Grove," and included the sites of Leeton and Chantilly. Known at different times as Rocky Run Mill, Cabell's Mill, Pittman's Mill, Middlegate, and Sandy Folly.

ORCHARD HILL . . . Built about 1740, the house has its original pine flooring and wide interior doors. Before extensive restoration and remodelling in the 1940's it had the small windows so typical of pioneer architecture. A partition was removed on the main floor, creating a living room with two large fireplaces. In the front yard stands a Ponderosa pine, "topped" by lightning a decade ago but still showing vigorous growth. On Braddock Road.

HAVENER HOUSE . . . Still owned by the Havener family, this was once an inn and during the Civil War was used as an aid station for the wounded. Opposite Methodist Church.

CENTREVILLE METHODIST CHURCH . . . The original church was built in 1855, destroyed during the Civil War, and rebuilt in 1870. The first church building, which was used as a hospital during the Battles of Bull Run, can be seen in this picture by the Civil War photographer Mathew Brady.

WAYSIDE RUIN . . . Within sight of the terminus of the world's first railroad built for military purposes, on the Murtaugh Farm, are the remnants of an ancient log cabin whose origin remains a mystery.

OLD AYRE HOUSE . . . Built about 1820, it is rumored to have been a residence for the manager of the vast Chantilly estate. It served as the first post office of Chantilly in 1830, was at one time a toll house, and was known as "Townsend's Wagon Stop". Before the house is a giant stone mounting block. The property was recently acquired by the International Town and Country Club. West of Fairfax City on Route 50.

CHANTILLY
AREA

GLENGYLE . . . Formerly known as "Roseville", this is a fine example of progressive building over a period of years, using various materials harmoniously. It combines sections of stone, brick and clapboard. Construction of the original stone portion was begun in 1790, but the tradition is that the superstitious owner would not allow it to be completed because of fear of death. Despite this, he died within a year. Although this home is actually in Loudoun County, it is considered a part of the Chantilly area.

MITCHELL'S TAVERN . . . This picturesque cottage was constructed of oak logs in 1803 as a tavern and used as a hospital after the Battle of Chantilly.

FRYING PAN PRIMITIVE BAPTIST CHURCH . . . At Floris, formerly called "Frying Pan", which took its name from a nearby stream, this old church was erected prior to 1800 on land granted for the purpose by "Councillor" Carter.

THE HERMITAGE . . . This house was originally called "Thornton's Tavern", and was at one time used as a post office for Centreville. The exact date of its construction is unknown. Three miles north of Centreville on Route 657.

SULLY . . . Erected in 1794 by Richard Bland Lee, first representative of Northern Virginia, whose vote determined the location of the Federal City. He was one of three Commissioners to superintend the reconstruction of the Federal buildings after the War of 1812. Because of his many responsibilities in public life he purchased a townhouse in Washington and sold Sully to a cousin, whose son, Rear Admiral Samuel Phillips Lee, married Elizabeth Blair. His town-house on Pennsylvania Avenue combined with the adjacent Blair House is now the Presidents' guest house. The Fairfax County Park Authority now maintains Sully as a museum. Located off Route 50 near Dulles Airport.

A SULLY DEPENDENCY . . . o
of the attractive plantation buildings.

LEETON . . . This is the ancestral home of the Turberville family, on which George Lee Turberville and his bride Harriot Lee (daughter of Richard Henry Lee, the "Signer") settled following their marriage in 1794, on land granted in 1727 to George Turberville of Hickory Hill, Westmoreland, County.

DULLES INTERNATIONAL AIRPORT . . . Dedicated by President John F. Kennedy in November, 1962, this magnificent facility for the Jet Age was designed by the late Eero Saarinen, one of the world's foremost architects. His concept of the "mobile lounge" enabled the Federal Aviation Agency to build a compact terminal heretofore impossible. The airport was named for Secretary of State John Foster Dulles, who between 1953 and 1959 flew nearly 600,000 miles during his service to the country.

**COURT HOUSE
RESTORATION** . . . In 1966 the original portion of the building was restored to its original design, which had undergone a number of changes in its one hundred sixty-six years of existence. Instead of the more recent two-story high windows, a double row of windows was reconstructed. Original fireplaces were uncovered. Monuments on the grounds include one to Captain John Quincy Marr, of the Warrenton Rifles, who was the first Confederate officer killed in action in the Civil War.

**FAIRFAX COUNTY COURTHOUSE** . . . The third courthouse since Fairfax County was established in 1742, the original portion shown was completed and in use by 1800. During the Civil War many records were lost, although occasionally a deed book is located and returned from some distant state. The first courthouse was located at Spring Field (now called Freedom Hill) and the second in Alexandria. The original wills of George and Martha Washington are on display in the present building. Civil War picture.

**FAIRFAX CITY**

BARBOUR HOUSE . . . Built about 1915 by John Strode Barbour, an attorney who moved to Fairfax from Culpeper in 1907. It was moved a block down the Ox Road in 1966, when purchased for office use by the law firm of McCandlish and Lillard. The house was originally constructed on land whereon had formerly stood the residence of Judge Henry Wirt Thomas, who was Lieutenant Governor of Virginia during the Civil War. A story is told by his descendants that the Judge had a favorite cat called "Blacknose", which had the habit of following him across the street to the Courthouse and sitting on the bench while his master heard cases. Another legend concerned a docile horse of broad dimensions named "Mosby", on whom four little children loved to ride. Because of his girth, the black-stockinged legs of the tikes stuck almost straight out, and some of the townspeople christened them, "The Spiders".

OLD TOWN HALL . . . Built in 1903 by Joseph Willard for the use of the citizens of the town of Fairfax, the Greek Revival structure houses the Huddleson Memorial Library. Dinners, plays, dances, and celebrations were held here for many years. Joseph Willard, of the Willard Hotel family, was a Lieutenant Governor of Virginia, and Ambassador to Spain during the Woodrow Wilson Administration.

EARP'S ORDINARY . . . Said to have been built around 1740, by the Earp family, this charming pink brick house is perhaps the oldest house in Fairfax. The community was called Earp's Corner before 1800, at which time the town of Providence came into being, later named Fairfax.

WILLCOXON TAVERN . . . The northwest corner of this old inn was mentioned in a survey to establish the Town of Providence, made in 1805 by Robert Ratcliffe. At various times a stagecoach stop and a trolley station, the large building was demolished in 1932 to clear the site for the building for the National Bank of Fairfax. The bricks and mantles from the old tavern were used in the building of Francis Pickens Miller's home on Chain Bridge Road at Oakton, now part of Flint Hill Private School.

BLENHEIM . . . Built from bricks made nearby for this building and Captain Rizin Willcoxon's Tavern, this home with impressive chimneys was occupied by Union soldiers during the Civil War, who left as mementoes many names carved on the walls of one of the upstairs rooms.

FIVE CHIMNEYS . . . This spacious house was erected in the 1880's by Richard Ratcliffe Farr using brick made on the place. Each of the five large chimneys has a cross worked into the design near the top.

ORCHARD DRIVE . . . This little house sits on part of the large tract which furnished many different kinds of fruit for the Willard Hotel Winery. There have been several different buildings housing the Willard Hotel in times past, and records indicate that the winery supplying them and this gardener's cottage were in existence by 1820. Rafters and joists include many large tree trunks in their original form.

TRURO RECTORY . . . The home of Dr. William Presley Gunnell in 1862 when Brigadier General Edwin H. Stoughton was captured by the daring Confederate guerrilla, John Singleton Mosby. Stoughton was in bed, and when awakened asked, "Have they taken Mosby?", to which the reply was, "Mosby has taken you."

VIENNA SKIRMISH . . . A railroad was used tactically for the first time in warfare during the Civil War. Four companies of the First Ohio Volunteers, riding in cars of the Loudoun and Hampshire Railway, were fired upon near Vienna in June, 1861. Seeing the superior forces of Confederates facing them, they scattered to the woods, stranded, as the frightened engineer ran the locomotive backwards all the way to Alexandria.

OAKTON SCHOOL . . . The first public school in Fairfax County, one room built in 1849, was known as "Flint Hill". It burned shortly after the Civil War and a new one was built facing the large oak tree at Hunter's Mill and Chain Bridge Roads. When Squire E. Smith applied for a community post office, he was advised that a Flint Hill already existed elsewhere. He therefore submitted the name "Oakton", after the large old tree shown in the picture with the second school.

FLINT HILL . . . Built in 1932 by famous author Helen Hill Miller, and named "Pickens Hill". It was constructed with bricks from the old Wilcoxon Tavern in Fairfax. Mantels from the old tavern were also used. It now forms the nucleus of Flint Hill Private School, on Chain Bridge Road at Interstate Route 66.

WOLF TRAP FARM PARK . . . A gift from Mrs. Jouett Shouse of Washington, D. C. Created by Act of Congress in 1966 as the first National Park for the Performing Arts. She also donated funds for an auditorium, known as the Filene Center, in honor of her parents, Mr. and Mrs. Lincoln Filene of Boston.

WINDOVER HEIGHTS . . . Fairfax County's best surviving example of Italian Villa style, built by Captain Harmon L. Saulsbury in 1869. On a clear day, Sugar Loaf Mountain in Maryland can be seen from the belvedere. Dr. Herbert Moody, a benefactor of the author O. Henry once lived here. Never-failing Saulsbury Spring is preserved in a park across the road. 224 Walnut Lane, Vienna.

ASH GROVE . . . The site of a hunting lodge built in 1750 by Bryan Fairfax, later the eighth Lord Fairfax, after whose family the County was named. His son, Thomas, who renounced the title of ninth Lord Fairfax, built the major portion of the house in the 1790's. Although partially burned in September of 1960, it has been repaired and restored by descendants of the Sherman family which bought it in 1850. In 1902, the family owned a pet peacock named "Sir Roger de Coverley" based on the fictional English country squire character and north country tune of the same name.

THE FALLS CHURCH
. . . Named after the Little Falls of the Potomac five miles away. The first services were held in the home of William Gunnell in the town. In 1733 Richard Blackburn of Rippon Lodge contracted to build a wooden church at this site. This was replaced in 1767-69 by a brick church erected under the supervision of the architect, Colonel James Wren of Longview. In 1775 the building was used as a recruiting station by Colonel Charles Broadwater, and during the Civil War as a hospital and later as a stable. Fairfax Street at Lee Highway.

LAWTON HOUSE . . .
Also known as "Lawton Manor", "Home Hill", and the "Old Buxton Place", the house was used as a headquarters during the Civil War by both sides. Built in the 1850's, it is an authentic example of architecture of the period and remains in its original setting, although the amount of acreage surrounding it has been greatly reduced. 203 Lawton Street, near Route 7.

CHERRY HILL . . . The exact date of the construction is uncertain although it has been estimated by an historical architect to have been built in the mid-1700's. It was used as a military hospital during the Civil War. Several live artillery shells have been found on the grounds, and beams in the old barn bear the names and service connections of soldiers. It was purchased by Joseph S. Riley in 1874 and was later the home of J. H. Riley, a noted ornithologist. The buildings and grounds will eventually become the property of the City of Falls Church. Adjacent to the City Hall.

## FALLS CHURCH
## AREA

FALLS CHURCH STATION . . . The establishment of both a railway and a trolley line were important factors in the development of Falls Church as a suburban home for Federal workers employed in Washington. Lee Highway at Fairfax Drive.

THE FALCON'S NEST . . . Formerly known as "Gum Aysle", the present name is based on the owner's family crest. The residence has undergone exterior changes which have given it a completely different appearance. The only interior change was the construction by a shipbuilder of a charming stairway fitted into a very small space in the living room to provide additional access to the upper floor. In the 300 block of South West Street.

BEFORE REMODELING . . . The original house was built about 1840 and was at one period owned by the Parker family.

CLOVERDALE . . . The land had originally been included in a tract granted to John Trammell on January 16, 1729. The construction date of the building is uncertain, but apparently quite early. The name derives from Williston Clover, who died in 1879 and willed the home to his widow, Delia. About 1950, when the stately old maple trees were cut down for the widening of Broad Street, this house, also in the path of construction, was moved one block away and turned to face Park Avenue. It has been made into offices and is presently owned by a descendant of John Gadsby of Alexandria and of the Munsons of Munson's Hill. 205 Park Avenue.

TAYLOR'S TAVERN . . . It was located on the Leesburg Turnpike on the northeast side of the present Seven Corners interchange. This old picture is from the National Archives.

THE BARN . . . located on Cameron Road in Greenway Downs, this unusual stone home was built around the wooden barn of "Oak Mount", home of Daniel French Dulaney, son of Benjamin Dulaney of "Shuter's Hill", Alexandria. Constructed of Falls Church pink granite from the quarry nearby, the interior reveals an inventive mind, with doors which slide up and down and an unusual stairway suspened from the ceiling by six large chains, patterned after the drawbridge at Chamaumont Castle in France.

FOUNTAIN OF FAITH . . . Designed by the Swedish sculptor, Carl Milles, the 38 bronze figures were twelve years in the making, cast in Sweden and shipped to National Memorial Park. Placed in different symbolic groups, the figures tell stories of faith and reunion. Lee Highway just outside of Falls Church.

HIGHLAND VIEW . . . The home of the late Edmund Flagg, noted lawyer, author and diplomat, it was built about 1870 in the Victorian manner.

# LEESBURG PIKE
# WEST TO LOUDOUN
# (ROUTE 7)

MOUNT PLEASANT . . . Built in 1770 by Colonel Robert Lindsay of The Mount for his son, Thomas. It descended to the prominent pioneer families of Swink and Shreve. During the Civil War Mosby's men often used it as a rendezvous. This fine old home was destroyed for the construction of Route 66.

LONGVIEW . . . Built in 1770 by Colonel James Wren, the only architect in the area at the time. He designed The Falls Church, Pohick Church and Christ Church in Alexandria. Northwest of Falls Church, off Shreve Road.

HANGMAN'S TREE . . . Although this majestic old oak may not actually have been used by Mosby as a gibbet, this is the local tradition. However, it was in the vicinity that Mosby's Peach Grove fight occurred. On the tree is a small bronze historical plaque which was placed upon it by the Daughters of the American Revolution. Destroyed 1968.

THE MOUNT . . . Built on a 400 acre tract in 1745 by Col. Robert Lindsay, whose family emigrated from Scotland to Northumberland County in the 1600's.

COLVIN RUN MILL . . . There was probably a mill on Colvill's Branch, now called Colvin Run, in the late 1700's but the present brick mill was probably built about 1820, close to Difficult Run. The Fairfax County Park Authority, which purchased the property in 1964, is restoring the mill and miller's house as a demonstration of the operation of merchants' mills which were so vital to early life in America.

MAYFIELD . . . Bought by Dr. William Day in 1840, at which time he enlarged the existing house. Mayfield was a surname in the Day family. He and his brother, Dr. John Day, who lived next door at "Ivy Chimney", delivered the babies and dispensed the pills to many residents of Fairfax and Loudoun Counties for decades, including the Civil War period. The interior of Mayfield boasts a wide staircase and a black marble mantle among its many handsome features.

DUNBARTON . . . This was considered an old house when purchased in 1830 by a Col. Coleman. There are several springs on the place, one of which has such a strong flow that it has never failed to supply water even during the worst droughts. It is located on the remains of an old county road shown on plats of 1742, off Seneca Road about one fourth mile from Route 7 in Dranesville. Central portion about 1750.

DRANESVILLE TAVERN . . . This hostelry was built no later than the early 1800's. It has also been known as the "Jackson Tavern" and is typical of early rural Virginia inns. Travelers to and from Alexandria and the Shenandoah Valley, as well as drovers on their way to the Georgetown and Washington markets, often stayed here. It is the last of perhaps seven taverns located in the Dranesville community at different times and is located on Sugarland Run, close to the site where the Colemans kept an ordinary at which George Washington frequently stopped.

THORNTON HOUSE . . . In 1852, Joshua Gunnell, acting for Reginald Fairfax, deeded almost 9,000 acres to Benjamin Thornton of Orange County, who built a fourteen-room Gothic Revival house near what was later called Thornton Station or Thornton's Mills on the Loudoun and Hampshire Railway.

AESCULAPIAN HOTEL . . . In 1886, Dr. Carl Adolph Max Wiehle bought more than 3,000 acres of the Thornton property. He established a town, "Wiehle", and employed a city planner from Germany to lay out a symmetrical Utopian town in the forest. An area along the railroad was reserved for industry and a thirty-five room hotel, the name of which means "medical center" in Greek, was built and became a popular summer resort. Dr. Wiehle died before his hope for a beautifully planned town could be realized.

E. DeLONG BOWMAN HOUSE . . . In 1923, the name of the Wiehle post office was changed to "Sunset Hills". The vast Wiehle acreage was acquired in 1927 by the Bowman family who in 1934 established a distillery thereon. The Bowman mansion has been made available as a social center for Reston.

RESTON STABLES . . . A New Town called Reston is being built on the old Wiehle property. The idea of town planning actually follows an early Virginia custom. Such Colonial towns as Williamsburg, Colchester and Alexandria were created on paper before any streets were laid out or buildings erected. By 1980 Reston is expected to be the home of 75,000 people. Within convenient walking distance for the residents are schools, golf courses, lakes, woodland trails, swimming pools, tennis courts, playgrounds, and a large stable appropriate to the Virginia hunt country.

LAKE ANNE AND HERON HOUSE . . . The town is close to Dulles International Airport and many industries are being developed in the park area set aside for them. The major architects for the community are Whittlesey & Conklin, Louis Sauer, Chloethiel W. Smith and Charles M. Goodman.

# Loudoun Heritage

FORMED in 1757 from land which had since 1742 comprised the western half of Fairfax County, Loudoun County was named after John Campbell, Lord Loudoun, a representative peer of Scotland who was appointed Governor of Virginia in 1756. As far as is known, he never set foot on Virginia soil and although he was later appointed a general his indecision and inefficiency caused Benjamin Franklin to say, "He is like little Saint George on the sign-boards; always on horseback, but never moves forward."

One of the first adventurers to navigate the Potomac River above the falls was the Swiss Baron Christopher de Graffenreid who had been granted permission to establish a German colony on the Shenandoah River. He was impressed with what he saw at the mouth of Goose Creek and wrote as follows, "There is in winter such a prodigious number of swans, geese and ducks on this river from Canavest (Conoy Island) to the Falls that the Indians make a trade of their feathers." That this situation had existed for many years is shown by the name the Indians used for the Potomac River above Great Falls. They called it "Cohongarooton", which means "Goose River", and English cartographers used that designation on their maps until after 1730.

Settlement of Loudoun began between 1720 and 1730, while the area was still part of Prince William County. The administration of Governor Gooch which began in 1727 ushered in a new era of religious tolerance for Virginia. The Church of England was still the Established Church, but dissenters were allowed to hold services and follow their tenets providing they registered their preaching points and location for their church buildings. As far as is known, Loudoun County never enforced the registration rule and people of all faiths moved into the area to settle it simultaneously and in harmony with their neighbors.

The people, who came from Pennsylvania, New Jersey and New York, were mostly farmers who tilled their own soil without the help of slaves. Their houses were small, and their tools and clothes were simple and few. "Shucking bees", which were contests to see how fast stacks of corn could be husked, and jigs and reels danced to a fiddler's tunes were favorite forms of recreation.

The Virginia planters who had come up from the south to settle large estates had many servants to do the work. Their main diversions consisted of visits to the mansions of friends where elaborate fancy-dress balls, fox hunts and tournaments continued for weeks.

The members of the Society of Friends, more familiarly known as Quakers, had learned their lessons well from their leader, William Penn. In a treatise published in London in 1684 directed to people emigrating to America he gave the following examples:

". . . I take my two men and go to my Lot . . . and then go to felling trees, proper to a first House, which will very well serve for the present occasion ,and afterwards be a good out House, till plenty will allow me to build a better . . . To build then, a House of thirty foot long and thirteen broad, with a partition neer the middle, and another to divide one end of the House into two small rooms, there must be eight Trees of about sixteen inches square, and cut off."

Although he was speaking of a frame house in the second instance, the idea was adapted to the fieldstone structures so typical of the early Quaker houses in Loudoun.

The Quakers settled in the Waterford and Leesburg areas. They were thrifty, honest and came to make homes where there was freedom of religious and moral thought, a good climate and a wholesome society of their compatriots.

Between 1730 and 1735, German settlers began to arrive from Pennsylvania and New York. They were peaceable, hard-working, orderly, and they clung to their own language, customs and habits. The Germans settled the northwest portion of the County in an organized body of sixty or more families recognizing the advantage of unity and numbers at a time when Indians were still a threat to the safety and lives of the settlers.

Of the English cavalier stock which settled on large tracts of land on the Potomac River and in the Middleburg area, John Esten Cooke eloquently wrote in 1883:

"The Virginian of the present time has ingrained in his character the cordial instincts and spirit of courtesy and hospitality which marked his ancestors. He has the English preference for the life of the country to the life of the city; is more at home among green fields and rural scenes than in streets; loves horses and dogs, breeds of cattle, the sport of fox-hunting, wood-fires, Christmas festivities, the society of old neighbors, political discussions, traditions of this or that local celebrity, and to entertain everybody to the extent of, and even beyond his limited means. Many of these proclivities have been laughed at, and the people have been criticized as provincial and narrow-minded; but after all it is good to love one's native soil, and to cherish the home traditions which give character to race. Of the Virginians it may be said that they have objected in all times to being rubbed down to a uniformity with all the rest of the world, and that they have generally retained the traits which characterized their ancestors."

After Braddock's defeat in 1755, during the French and Indian War, Indians attacked many settlements in the Shenandoah Valley, and surviving refugees crossed the Blue Ridge to settle in the western part of Loudoun County. About the same time, fact and fiction led to the nick-naming of the well-travelled road variously known as the Carolina Road, the Shenandoah Hunting Path and the Plain Path, now Route 15. It was once a well-defined Iroquois trail and the western limit of European settlement set by a treaty in 1684. Like the Great North Road of England, the long, lonely route fell heir to many stories true and imaginary about highwaymen who relieved drovers of their stock and other possessions. It was said of a Gentleman Rogue, "Captain Harper", who lived in the shadow of the Bull Run Mountains, that he took from the rich and gave to the poor like the legendary Robin Hood. The road was for these reasons referred to as the "Rogue's Road".

The Loudoun County Courthouse was begun by Aeneas Campbell in 1758, on two lots of the lands of Nicholas Minor, keeper of the Ordinary and owner of the plantation which he called "Fruitlands." It was located near the crossing of the Alexandria-Keys Gap Highway and the Carolina Road, the spot where the present courthouse stands. A fort and a few log houses had stood at the intersection for some years before, and the little settlement had been called George Town after George the Second. When the county seat was officially established, it was named Leesburg. It is not clear for what Lee the town was named. Thomas Lee of Stratford had been an extensive landholder in the area; his sons, Philip Ludwell and Francis Lightfoot, were trustees of the town; Francis Lightfoot Lee was also presiding justice, county lieutenant, and burgess. Charles Binns was the first county clerk, and he and his son by the same name, who succeeded him in the job, served a total of eighty years in that capacity. Aeneas Campbell of Raspberry Plain was first sheriff, and the first county surveyor was George West, Gent.

When the Revolutionary War broke out, Josias Clapham, Thomas Mason and Leven Powell very actively supported the cause of independence. John Champe was a young soldier from the vicinity of what is now Aldie, and was asked by "Light-Horse Harry" Lee to desert to the British and effect a capture of Benedict Arnold. Unfortunately, plans went awry when the British left by ships for the lower part of Virginia on the same day Champe was to have made the capture.

There is a legend that in August, 1814, many of the Federal Papers were stored for safekeeping at Rokeby near Leesburg for two weeks when the British were in the Washington area during the War of 1812.

James Monroe began the building of Oak Hill while he was President and retired there after his term in office. He and the whole County were hosts to Lafayette on his famous return visit to America in 1825. The General had been only twenty years of age when appointed in 1777 during the American Revolution. He was honored by parades, wined and dined, speeches were made by notables, including Ludwell Lee (who had been Lafayette's aide-de-camp), and an estimated ten thousand people paid homage to the Frenchman.

A detailed map of the county was first drawn in 1853 by a Quaker, Yardley Taylor, who was the County Surveyor at the time. On it were noted locations of various natural resources and the map was accompanied by a brief history of the county written by Taylor.

The magnitude of a plantation complex is described in a newspaper advertisement placed by General Rust offering his property of 1,720 acres for sale in 1856. "The dwelling of fine stone and brick, 120 feet in front (he modestly underestimated by twelve feet) . . . all necessary outbuildings of brick . . . comfortable quarters for at least 50 servants . . . brick carriage house for the stabling of at least 40 horses."

War clouds gathered once again in 1861, sharply dividing the County because of the division of allegiances. Although most sided with the South, there were two companies of soldiers called the Loudoun Rangers who served in the Union Army, and thus there were times when brother fought brother and friend was pitted against friend. Three forts named Evans, Johnston and Beauregard were constructed around Leesburg but the the need to use them never arose. Nearby, the Battle of Ball's Bluff was fought in October, 1861, resulting in the killing or wounding of almost a thousand Federal troops and less than two hundred Confederates in a poorly supported offensive by the Union on an almost impregnable objective. Oliver Wendell Holmes Jr. was wounded there, but lived to become a great jurist of the Supreme Court. The National Park Service maintains its smallest National Cemetery at the site.

Loudoun was the headquarters of Colonel E. V. White's Laurel Brigade, named for the jaunty evergreen sprigs they wore in their hatbands, and John Singleton Mosby's guerrilla warfare tactics were so effective in the area that the Union had to maintain a large force in Northern Virginia because of his constant harassment of wagon trains, railroads and small war parties. Many details were sent out by the Union to get Mosby, dead or alive, but they all failed. Mosby continued his effective work and the domain in which he and his Partisan Rangers operated came to be known as "Mosby's Confederacy". It included territory in both Loudoun and Fauquier Counties. The boundaries were described thus:

"From Snickersville (now Bluemont) along the Blue Ridge Mountains to Linden; thence to Salem (now Marshall); to The Plains; thence along the Bull Run Mountains to Aldie and from thence along the turnpike to the place of beginning, Snickersville."

Mosby's method of operation explains why so many families say that he or his men had been hidden in the family home one or more times during the Civil War. They had no definite headquarters, for that would have invited capture. When they were being pursued, they scattered and hid in the woods, farmhouses or even masqueraded as farmers. Mosby was a lawyer by training and experience and stoutly maintained that his guerrilla tactics were within the rules of warfare. When the famous "Greenback Raid" was made on a Baltimore and Ohio train at Brown's Crossing, Mosby divided up the two payrolls being carried on it among his men, and from then until the end of the war there was said to be a good supply of Federal currency circulating in Loudoun.

It took many years for the County to recover from the ravages of the Civil War. Improved highways and the completion of the Alexandria, Loudoun and Hampshire Railroad to Bluemont from Leesburg, where it had been halted by the War, had a good effect on commerce and encouraged many new families, some of them former Union servicemen, to settle in the County. The fertility of the land soon reestablished Loudoun as an excellent farming and grazing area.

Many of the place names have changed in Loudoun. In addition to these already mentioned, Lincoln was formerly called Goose Creek; Ryan was called Five Points; Ashburn was called Farmwell; Waterford was called Milltown; Lovettsville was first called Thrasher's Store and then New Town. Middleburg was so named because it was halfway between Winchester and Alexandria.

As the old stone houses were usually put up and then mortared with a mixture of mud and lime, repairs had occasionally to be made when holes would appear. The former owner of Derry's Tavern, which is located near Hillsboro, used to counter complaints from his visitors about his drafty house with the assurance that although the wind blew in, they were not to worry as "it always blew right on out". He also resisted installation of central heating as it couldn't possibly warm him three times as his wood did; once when he cut it, once when he carried it in the house, and once when he burned it.

BROAD RUN . . . On Route 7, originally called the Ridge Road, then the Alexandria to Leesburg Turnpike, one can see the old toll house and double-arch stone bridge which were built about 1800.

## OUT THE PIKE, TO LEESBURG

ROLLING ROAD'S ROCK RAINBOW . . . West of Dranesville, the banks of Sugarland Run eroded from the old stone bridge, leaving a shell of masonry which collapsed during the winter of 1963. This was one of the routes along which hogsheads of tobacco were drawn by oxen.

LOG CABIN . . . This pioneer home stood across the road from the toll house until about 1960.

BELMONT . . . Built in 1799 by Ludwell Lee on land patented in 1728 by his grandfather, Thomas Lee of Stratford, and inherited by his first wife, Flora Lee, who was his first cousin. Ludwell Lee was aide-de-camp to General Lafayette during the campaign of 1781 and entertained him at Belmont in 1825.

JANELIA . . . On a large successfully operating farm, stands this handsome Norman mansion with six tall chimneys. Remnants of a mysterious old park-type wall of large boulders winds its way through part of the property. Located toward the Potomac off Route 7 six miles east of Leesburg.

LEESBURG

THOMAS BALCH LIBRARY . . . The library building was given to the community by the sons of Thomas Balch, who was born in Leesburg. Located on West Market Street, the library also is the headquarters of the Loudoun County Historical Society. Mr. Balch, who was serving as Acting Consul at Paris, witnessed the battle between the ships, Alabama and Kearsarge, off Cherbourg on June 19, 1864. The following year he suggested in a letter to the New York Tribune, the settlement of the Alabama claims through arbitration. The claims were settled in 1872 by an international court of arbitration.

LOUDOUN COUNTY COURTHOUSE . . . First open for court in 1895 on the site of two previous courthouses. The Confederate statue is the work of William Sebier, the famous sculptor of the Virginia Group at the Gettysburg Battlefield.

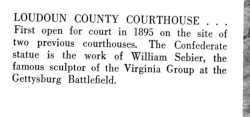

LAUREL BRIGADE INN . . . This charming inn, which serves excellent food, was given its name in honor of the brigade of Stuart's Cavalry which included the 6th Virginia Cavalry, recruited from Loudoun and adjoining counties. Their members were identified by a sprig of laurel worn in their hat-bands. The stone building was erected between 1796 and 1817 on the site of Nicholas Minor's wooden tavern which dated back to 1755 when General Braddock's men under Sir Peter Halkett's command stopped there en route to Fort Duquesne. One block west of the Courthouse.

THE FENDALL HOUSE . . . Now a charming residence, this was formerly Osburn's Tavern, built about 1795. Lafayette was "tendered a sumptuous banquet" here during his visit to Leesburg according to a newspaper dated August 9, 1825. 109 Loudoun Street.

OLD TAVERN . . . Presently used as a doctor's office, it was originally an early tavern. Drawings on the third floor walls are attributed to Hessian soldiers after the Revolution. In the 100 block of Loudoun Street.

GEORGE WASHINGTO[N]
HEADQUARTERS . . .
oldest house in Leesbur[g]
was the headquarters o[f]
Peter Halkett prior to
battle of the Mononga[hela]
during the French
Indian Wars. (On this [ex]
dition George Washin[gton]
was a volunteer aid
camp.) Henry Clay, w[hile]
campaigning for the P[resi-]
dency in 1831, signed
name on the wall.

OLD STONE CHURCH . . . The first deeded
Methodist property in America was this site
bought from Nicholas Minor, May 11, 1766, upon
which was erected the Nation's first church of this
denomination. The photograph was taken in 1892,
two years after close of regular services in the
building. It was sold in 1900 for $416.05 and
demolished.

THE COX HOUSES . . . The house on the left
was built just after the Revolution, with two later
additions, completed about 1822. Next door is a
town house built before 1800 and used for many
years as a law office.

**SHENSTONE RESTORED**
. . . The property was deeded by Ferdinando Fairfax to Benjamin Grayson before 1787 and the house was used by the miller who operated Dry Mill. Architecturally it has a different design from most of Loudoun's stone houses. Adapted to a steep hillside, the kitchen and dining room are on the ground level, the living room and two bedrooms on the second floor, with the usual sleeping loft above, approached on worn stairs with marbelized paint still showing on the risers. Two miles west of Leesburg.

**MOUNTAIN GAP SCHOOL . . .**
Located on an acre of property purchased from James Adams and his wife for $30.00 in 1885, this little red schoolhouse was an early alma mater for many Loudoun County residents. The deed description provides for 300 feet along the road on one side, and the top of Hog Back Mountain on the other. In 1953, the school was bought at auction by Wilbur Hall of Leesburg, and restored with appropriate furnishings. Located on Route 15, five miles south of Leesburg.

**SALT BOX HOUSE . . .** A charming new home erected about 1963; an authentic reproduction of a Colonial New England "salt box house", identified by its central chimney and typical roofline. Its name is derived from the similarity in shape to an old-fashioned wall container for salt.

— 119 —

LOUDOUN HUNT . . .
A rider and hounds with
Woodburn Plantation in
the background.

WOODBURN
PLANTATION

MANSION HOUSE . . .
Built in 1820. Located
four miles from Leesburg
off Route 15, west on
Route 704.

SIDE VIEW OF WOODBURN . . .

WOODBURN . . . This plantation is of particular importance because all of its main buildings are preserved, reflecting the development of a country estate starting from the frontier period. Early nick-named "Dr. Nixon's Folly", since he spent his wealth in the development of the estate. In addition to the buildings shown in these pictures are a brick spring house and a stone stable.

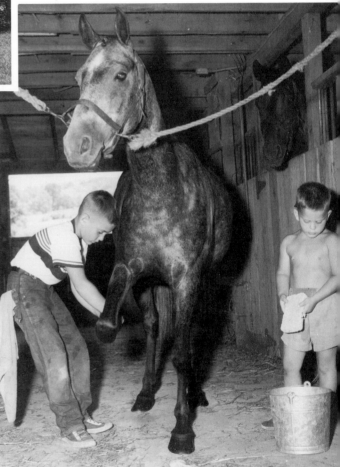

PREPARING FOR A HORSESHOW . . .
On a Loudoun estate.

WOODBURN BARN . . . Made from bricks burned on the place in 1800.

MILLER'S COTTAGE . . . This small stone house bears a 1787 date.

# WOODBURN PLANTATION

LOG CABIN . . . The earliest date on the plantation, 1747, is found in a stone wall of this cabin, used as a tenant house. An iron heat reflector in the basement fireplace has the inscription VIRGA 1737.

THE MILL . . . This grist mill bears the date of 1777.

ROKEBY . . . Pre-Revolutionary brick house was originally similar to Kenmore in exterior architectural design, extensively altered in the early 1900's and again in the late 1950's. According to tradition, the Declaration of Independence and the Constitution were brought here for safekeeping in the basement vault for about two weeks in August, 1814, when the British entered Washington during the War of 1812. (Also, see page 153.)

ESTATES
NEAR
LEESBURG

DODONA MANOR . . . Original portion built prior to 1825. George Washington Ball, a great-nephew of General Washington, purchased it from his brother Fayette Ball in 1855. In 1941 it became the home of General and Mrs. George C. Marshall.

MORVEN PARK . . .
Built about 1825 by Thomas Swann, Senior, who married Ann Byrd Page. He was president of the Valley Bank in Leesburg and trained the lawyer Wirt for whom Wirt Street in Leesburg was named. The home was extensively enlarged by Thomas Swann, Junior, **Governor of Maryland** during the Civil War. It was purchased in 1903 by Westmoreland Davis who later became Governor of Virginia. His remains are buried in a vault in the garden. The estate was opened to the public in late 1967, under the management of the Westmoreland Davis Memorial Foundation. Includes The Winmill Antique Carriage Museum.

THROUGH THE GARDEN GATE . . . This famous boxwood garden of several acres was planted at Morven Park by Governor Davis.

EXETER . . . Erected between 1796 and 1800 by Dr. Wilson Cary Selden on land inherited by his wife, a member of the Mason family. An elaborate social event which took place here in 1843 was the marriage of his granddaughter to John Augustine Washington, a great-nephew of the General. Three years later the property was sold to General George Rust who erected a large addition in 1854. Horatio Trundle is said to have bought Exeter in 1857. The main portion of this brick house appears to be frame because of weatherboard facing across the front. Of special interest architecturally is the harmonious use of several styles of roofs.

## NORTH TOWARD
## THE POTOMAC

LOCUST HILL . . . The oldest portion dates to the late 1700's with later additions. The portico, a replica of President Jackson's home, The Hermitage, was part of the reviewing stand at the Second Inaugural of President Franklin D. Roosevelt.

SELMA . . . Original home built before 1800 by Armistead Thomson Mason, locally known as the "Chief of Selma". Mason was killed in 1819 in a duel with his cousin, Colonel John Mason McCarty of adjacent "Raspberry Plain". The estate was later owned by several generations of the Beverley family and purchased in 1896 by Elijah Viers White II. He built the present mansion and was at one time decorated by the French Government for his skill in the breeding of Percheron horses.

A PLANTATION GATEWAY . . .

ROCKLAND . . . Built in 1822 by General George Rust on land bought in 1817 from Burgess Ball for whose family nearby Ball's Bluff is named, the site of a famous Civil War battle. Rockland is named for the picturesque outcroppings of limestone which extend through the garden. The estate remains in possession of the Rust family.

RASPBERRY PLAIN . . . The land was granted by the Proprietor in 1731 to Joseph Dixon who probably built the first house. In 1754 he sold the property to Aeneas Campbell, later the first sheriff of Loudoun County who is said to have had a small jail and ducking stool on the place. Thomson Mason, younger brother of George Mason IV of Gunston Hall, bought the estate in 1760 and built a new house in 1771 on the site of the present mansion which was erected by John G. Hopkins in the early 1900s.

WHITE'S FERRY . . . Also known at one time as Conrad's Ferry, this is the last existing ferry on the Potomac River. It is off Route 15 north of Leesburg, on county route 655.

MONTRESOR . . . About 1750, William Douglass came to Loudoun County from Scotland, served as a justice in 1770, a Colonel in the Revolutionary War, and sheriff in 1782. He owned the estates of Garalland and Montresor. In the late 1800's Montresor was acquired by Colonel Elijah V. White, who commanded a battalion in the Laurel Brigade. He was the father of the owner of Selma. The estate is now operated as a private summer camp.

CHESTNUT HILL . . . Built on land acquired in 1739 by Josias Clapham, a justice and member of the Assembly and the Revolutionary Conventions. He was an original trustee of Leesburg, founded in 1758 and Middleburg founded in 1787. The original portion of the existing house was built by his grandson Samuel about 1800, enlarged about 1812. It came into the Mason family through marriage and for some years the original draft of Virginia's Declaration of Rights by George Mason remained in their possession, now in the Library of Congress. Near Point of Rocks.

BIG SPRING . . . On Route 15, 2.4 miles north of Leesburg, the spring breaks forth from an underground stream a few feet from the highway.

NOLAND'S FERRY . . .
Although the ferry is no longer in existence, its name is perpetuated in the home built about 1775 and left uncompleted. The house was handsomely restored in the early 1950's by Mr. and Mrs. W. G. Brookins including the fine boxwood garden. Philip Noland purchased the land in 1724 from George Slater. He married Elizabeth, daughter of Francis Awbrey who operated a ferry near Georgetown. Noland petitioned the Assembly for a license to run a ferry in 1748, but Josias Clapham's petition pre-dated his six years. Although both ran ferries for most of the ensuing years, their rivalry wasn't officially settled until 1779, at which time a license was issued to Philip Noland's son Thomas.

HUNTING HILL . . .
Perhaps the oldest of the Quaker stone houses in Loudoun which are still in good condition. The builder is thought to have been Richard Brown, who erected it about 1737 and in 1784 sold it to Thomas Taylor, for whom Taylorstown was named. The large fireplaces, small windows and low ceilings reveal the practical methods for keeping a house comfortably warm in the days before central heating. Interior walls are of pine panelling or of whitewashed plaster made of mud and animal hair.

WILLARD HALL . . . When Doctor Dan Willa[rd]
of Ohio was stationed in Lovettsville during t[he]
Civil War, the Old Reform Church was used as [a]
hospital. Across the street was a charming p[re-]
Revolutionary house which so enchanted him t[hat]
he returned and purchased it after the war.

TAYLORSTOWN MILL . . . Built in the late 1700's
in a community named after Thomas Taylor of
Hunting Hill.

FARM SCENE NEAR
WATERFORD . . .

WATERFORD,
THE VILLAGE
TIME FORGOT

RUSTIC DESIGN . . .
Weather - silvered wood
and rusted iron.

THE OLD MILL . . . In 1943 the Waterford Foundation was established to encourage restoration of old homes and buildings in Waterford and to stimulate a revival of arts and handicrafts. The Waterford Homes Tour and Crafts Exhibit is held the first week of October each year, attended by thousands of visitors. The original mill was of logs and across the stream from this, which is the third structure. The community was first called Milltown, but was renamed by the town's cobbler Thomas Moore who came to America from Waterford, Ireland. Amos Janney, who came from Bucks County, Pennsylvania about 1730 is thought to have built the first mill and a portion of the present one, about 1740. Asa Moore built the first house.

FRIENDS' MEETING HOUSE . . . This group of Friends was organized in 1733 and erected this building in 1775 which served as a place of worship and a civic center until 1929, when it became a private residence. Nearby is the early cemetery.

STREET SCENE . . .                                          A LOG HOUSE . . .

PARKER-BENNETT HOUSE . . . Originally two houses. The one on the left was built in 1835 by Ephraim Schooley, and the one on the right, using the common wall between them, was built in 1850-56 by James W. McKinney. The name notes the two families who dwelt there for the longest period of time. John G. Lewis restored the buildings in 1959 and combined them into one residence by cutting through the common wall.

ARCH HOUSE . . . Built about 1763, this building was free from taxation for many years because the town's fireladders were stored in the archway which was constructed to allow free access to its well, then the town's best source of drinking water. This home was restored by Edward and Leroy Chamberlin.

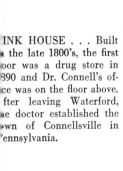

INK HOUSE . . . Built
in the late 1800's, the first
floor was a drug store in
1890 and Dr. Connell's office was on the floor above.
After leaving Waterford,
the doctor established the
town of Connellsville in
Pennsylvania.

ARNOLD GROVE METHODIST CHURCH . . . Built in 1830 on land received from Michael and Christine Arnold, the church maintains a charming simplicity to this day. Located on Route 9 east of Hillsboro.

SALEM CHURCH . . . Located in Neersville near Route 9, this church and a little stone schoolhouse nearby were built in 1833.

## HILLSBORO
## TO HARPERS FERRY

HILLSBORO has an important claim to fame as the birthplace of Susan Koerner in 1831, the mother of Wilbur and Orville Wright, inventors of the airplane.

When General Lafayette was wounded in the leg in the battle of Brandywine, James Crook who later settled near Hillsboro rescued him, and in so doing, was also wounded. Both men were treated by Dr. Gustavus Brown Horner of Fauquier County of whom Lafayette inquired during a touching reunion upon meeting James Crook at Leesburg.

WHITESTONE . . . This attractive stone house was restored by John G. Lewis of Hamilton. It was built on land bought by Francis Awbrey in 1750, sold to John Taylor in 1760, and to James McIlhaney in 1765, who is thought to have been the builder. Located two miles outside of Hillsboro on Route 9.

APPALACHIAN TRAIL . . . The Trail, which follows the crest of the mountains from Maine to Georgia passes through Virginia in which there are four shelters for the hikers donated by Senator Harry F. Byrd, Sr. He dedicated "Byrd's Nest No. 4" in June of 1965 and many times participated in camping and hiking trips at home and abroad.

PAEONIAN SPRINGS . . . A charming small community located in an area of springs, the largest being upon the Chanbourne estate, where the fine water was commercially bottled in the late 1800's. The village was a small health spa around the turn of the century. The oldest structure in the area is probably the Pierpont home which remains in the family's possession. It was built about 1763 by Obed Pierpont, who lies buried in the Quaker cemetery at nearby Waterford. On Route 9, between Leesburg and Waterford.

HARPERS FERRY . . . Once a part of Virginia, Peter Stephens was the first settler, in 1733. It was first called "Peter's Hole", but the name was changed in 1747 when Robert Harper bought the property and established a ferry and a mill. The National Park Service maintains the Harpers Ferry National Monument there, and a park leads from Jefferson Rock to Loudoun Heights where it meets the Appalachian Trail. Virginia is in the foreground of the picture with West Virginia across the Potomac to the left and Maryland across the Shenandoah to the right.

— 135 —

BIG ROCK . . . Sometimes referred to as the Old Hoge Place, this stone house was built about 1790. It is located near Hughesville at the foot of Mount Gilead.

PURCELLVILLE - HAMILTON
AREA

RANDOM WIDTH CLAPBOARDS . . . This charming house was built in 1847 or earlier, by Asa M. Janney on two acres purchased from James Heaton Purcell. It was part of the 533 acre tract granted 1748 to Mahlon Kirkbride of Bucks County, Pennsylvania, inherited by his grandson, Stacey Taylor, from whose estate Purcell acquired it. The deed describes a "small frame house built between two large fieldstone chimneys."

MINOR BARTLOW HOUSE . . . Built in 1785 by Minor Bartlow for Blackstone Janney, this brick and fieldstone house was skillfully restored in 1963 by John G. Lewis. The interesting dependencies include a stone smokehouse, springhouse, and a barn with a high stone foundation. The dining room has beaded beams and a cooking fireplace. Located near Hamilton.

KETOCTIN BAPTIST CHURCH... The present building was constructed in 1854 on the site of three previous churches, two of log and one of stone. The first was built about 1756 by John Garrard on land conveyed by Nicholas Osburn for two shillings, six pence and a yearly rental of one ear of Indian corn. At the crossroads of Routes 711 and 716, two miles north of Purcellville.

OAKLAND GREEN . . . An excellent living text in Loudoun architectural history. This house was built by the Quaker Richard Brown in three stages. The first, of logs, was built about 1737, the second of stone about 1741 and the third of brick about 1790. It is still owned by his descendants.

## LINCOLN AREA

GOOSE CREEK MEETING HOUSE . . . Also called the Old Quaker Meeting House, this stone building which is now a private residence was built about 1770, near the site of an earlier log church constructed about 1747. The present brick church and schoolhouse across the road were built about 1817.

## SILCOTT SPRINGS AREA

SILCOTT SPRINGS FARM . . . The stone house (not pictured) was probably built about 1791. In the 1800's the estate became a spa noted for its fine mineral waters. The excellent stone barn is dated 1807 and noteworthy for the quoined corners which are typical of the masonry construction of the area.

WILLOW GREENS . . . It is obvious that the
three sections of this house were built at
different periods; the chimney of the center
section bears the date of 1791. The original
builder was Timothy Taylor, a Quaker from
Bucks County, Pennsylvania.

EARLY BRIDGE . . . Spanning Beaver Dam
Creek on the Little River—Snickers Gap Turnpike, a toll road which was chartered in 1810
and completed before 1816. Southeast of
Philomont on Route 734 near the crossing
of 731.

STONELEIGH FARM MILKHOUSE . . .
The oldest part of the main house now used as
a kitchen wing, was built about 1800. The
newer wing was added in 1852 by Mason
James who carved his initials and date on a
stone near the roof. The old milk house interior is many feet below ground level, and
stone-lined for coolness. Nearby are the ruins
of an icehouse quite deep. The estate was
formerly called Mount Silvia.

## ROUND HILL AREA

OLD STONE UNDERPASS . . . Where the
viaduct at Clark's Gap, built by the Alexandria, Loudoun and Hampshire Railway Company shortly after the Civil War, passes under
the Leesburg Pike, Route 7.

TIPPITT'S HILL . . . Used as a wagon stop for teams from about 1735. Foundations of an old smithy and a stone barn may still be seen. V. V. Purcell, who added six rooms in 1910, worked with his son to establish a commercial orchard, and many people from the Washington area have journeyed to Round Hill at harvest time to pick their own fruit and berries.

GARDENER'S HOUSE . . . One of the dependencies of the Yatton farm, it is built against a hillside with the roofline of a New England saltbox house, unusual in this area.

OATLANDS . . . The estate was cut from a 63,000 acre tract granted by Lord Fairfax to Robert "Councillor" Carter of Nomini in 1776. His son, George, built the stately mansion about 1800 and laid out the gardens. The mansion and grounds were recently given to the National Trust for Historic Preservation by Mrs. David E. Finley and Mrs. Eustis Emmet and are open to the public.

## SOUTH OF LEESBURG
## (ROUTE 15)

OATLANDS GARDEN . . . An excellent example of early Virginia landscape design, on a wooded hillside. At focal points are fountains, gates of delicate ironwork and other ornaments.

SHADOW MOUNTAIN
. . . A residence of great charm created from one of the traditional stone farm houses, central portion of which was erected prior to 1810 by Peter Carr. It is situated in a beautiful grove of trees in the shadow of Hog Back Mountain, with a stone springhouse at the foot of the lawn on the banks of a stream.

OAK HILL . . . While President James Monroe was in office he began the construction of this home. It was designed by Thomas Jefferson and James Hoban with William Benton supervising the building. Trees were given to the President by Congressmen of each state and two of the marble mantels were gifts from Lafayette in appreciation for the hospitality he had received at Oak Hill. The estate was later owned by Henry Fairfax, a member of the State Legislature whose hobby was the raising of hackney horses. A later owner, Frank C. Littleton, enlarged the mansion in 1923 in accordance with original plans which had never been completed. He had the patio paved with sandstone slabs quarried on the estate which have imprints of the tracks of dinosaurs.

ALDIE MILL . . . A good mill-site often determined the location of a pioneer settlement and this was the case with Aldie. Two manor houses above the village look down upon the mill, a miller's house and a roadside house which was probably an early ordinary and which were the earliest buildings of the village. They date to the late 1770s and early 1800s.

ALDIE

THE MILLER'S HOUSE . . . Now a charming residence in a setting of fine trees at the foot of the Bull Run Mountains with a garden extending to the stream.

— 144 —

THE MERCER HOUSE
Originally called Aldie Manor, from which the village was given its name in 1810, it was named for Aldie Castle in Scotland by the builder, Charles Fenton Mercer. Mercer, 1758-1857, was a member of the Virginia House of Delegates, a Brigadier General in the War of 1812 and a member of Congress.

PEMBERTON . . . Built by Colonel William Berkeley in 1778 and later the home of William Noland Berkeley whose poetry is inscribed with a date of 1835 on a window pane.

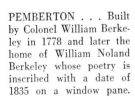

WOODBYRNE . . . A handsome white house directly above the road as one enters Aldie, the rear portion of which is a much older log cabin. The livingroom is now floored with mellow old boards which the present owners brought down from the attic, the original floors having been worn through.

THE STONE BRIDGE... This is one of the few old stone bridges in Virginia still in use. It spans the Little River for which the Turnpike was named. The river is actually quite a small tributary of Goose Creek which flows into the Potomac.

NARROWGATE . . . This attractive house of Flemish bond brick abuts on the road, which suggests that it may have originally been an ordinary. The wooden addition on the east side was made for Aldie's first postmistress just before the Civil War. There is a tradition that during the conflict a Confederate prisoner escaped disguised as a woman. The old smokehouse is preserved in the garden.

## ALDIE
## TO MIDDLEBURG

DOVER . . . Toward Middleburg from Aldie one passes this fine old Flemish bond brick house which was built in 1790. It has had no modifications except for the addition of modern conveniences and maintenance. It was for a period the Dover English and Classical School.

OAKHAM . . . Built in 1830 in an oak forest on the Peyton land grant by Colonel Hamilton Rogers whose daughter, Mary, married Colonel John Fairfax. The estate remains in the possession of the Fairfax family. Among its treasures is a game table presented by Lafayette to James Monroe.

WAYSIDE COTTAGE... Across the road from Dover is this picturesque little cottage.

RED FOX TAVERN . . .
Built on land first owned by Joseph Chinn at Chinn's Crossroads which was renamed Middleburg when incorporated in 1787. First called Chinn's Ordinary when it was built in 1728, the site was acquired by Leven Powell when he laid out the town, and later sold to Noble Beveridge. It has also been known as the Middleburg Inn and the Mansion House, and is still a delightful place to dine.

## MIDDLEBURG

COLONIAL INN . . .
Across the street from the Red Fox Tavern, it was built by the same Noble Beveridge and is also still dispensing southern hospitality.

## MIDDLEBURG
## AND BEYOND

TRINITY EPISCOPAL CHURCH . . .
In nearby Upperville, Fauquier County.
This beautiful edifice is a gift to the congregation from Paul Mellon.

FOXCROFT . . . In 1914,
Miss Charlotte Haxall Noland founded a school for
girls on an estate of six
hundred acres in a valley
between the Cobbler and
Bull Run Mountains. The
original building, called
"The Brick House" is
thought to be the oldest
dwelling built of the material in Loudoun County.
There is a legend that
Mary Ball visited relatives
there before she married
George Washington's
father, and it is in her
honor that the boxwood
garden is named.

ALONG THE LOUDOUN-FAUQUIER LINE

FARMER'S DELIGHT . . . Center portion of present house was started in 1771 by James Lane, sheriff of Loudon County and a vestryman of the parish. It was completed in 1781. Colonel Joseph Lane, an officer in the Army during the Whiskey Rebellion is buried in the family cemetery. Grounds developed by the present owners include a twelve acre lake, and a log cabin originally built in Leesburg about 1750, which has been transported to the present site on the lake.

VINE HILL . . . Erected in 1804 by a Mr. Cochran, this fine old house on an 8 acre site has been recently restored for use as an office for THE CHRONICLE OF THE HORSE, with a fireproof underground vault for THE NATIONAL SPORTING LIBRARY. An excellent example of a preservation adaptation.

BENTON . . . Built in 1830 by William Benton, masterbuilder who erected many of the finest estate homes in Loudoun County including Oak Hill, Huntlands and probably Woodburn. Near Leesburg.

CATESBY . . . Extensive gardens include the beautifully planted forecourt, a woodland path, pool, dovecote, terraced green garden, rose garden and box allees that form a background for several pieces of outstanding sculpture. Greenhouses and conservatory are filled with a fine collection of rare flowers and orchids.

OAK SPRING . . . Near Upperville, but in Fauquier County. The present estate combines the Oak Spring property acquired in the early 1800's by Robert Fletcher, and Rokeby, purchased in 1825 by Nathaniel Lufborough; both being part of the Landon Carter grant of 9,699 acres from Lord Fairfax in 1731. This Rokeby should not be confused with the estate near Leesburg or the Rokeby to which Dolley Madison fled seeking refuge at the home of her friend, Matilda Lee Love, in Fairfax County near the Little Falls of the Potomac, which was destroyed before the Civil War.

AYRSHIRE . . . The house was completed in 1914 by General James Buchanan who kept one of the largest and best thoroughbred horse breeding establishments in Virginia.

HUNTLANDS GARDENS
. . . Here may be found
serpentine brick walls similar to those at the Uni-
versity of Virginia. A
portion of these bricks
came from a house in
Leesburg which was des-
troyed to prepare a site
for the construction of a
theater with a parking lot.

HUNTLANDS . . . Ori-
ginal house built about
1830 by William Benton.
Joseph Thomas, Master of
Foxhounds of the Pied-
mont Hunt, added the two
wings in 1911 and trans-
formed it into an English-
type estate. The stables
are replicas of those on the
estate of the Duke of
Beaufort in England.

THE PIEDMONT HUNT
. . . Of Loudoun and
Fauquier Counties. This is
the oldest hunt club in
Virginia.

WELBOURNE . . . In this
fine old home among the
original heirloom portraits
is that of Colonel Richard
Dulany. In 1853 he
founded the Upperville
Colt and Horse Show, the
first of its kind in the
country, still held annually
at the original site.

# Fauquier Heritage

FOUR petitions were required in the Assembly before the "back inhabitants" of Hamilton parish were successful in creating a new county. Efforts which began in 1755 were thwarted at one time by Loudoun and Fairfax Counties, which wished to divide the territory under consideration rather than have it become a separate entity. In 1759, however, a new county called "Fauquier" was created from the southwest portion of Prince William County. It was named after Francis Fauquier, who was appointed lieutenant governor of Virginia in 1758. His father, Dr. John Fauquier had fled France to avoid religious persecution, married an Englishwoman, Elizabeth Chamberlayne, and eventually became a director of the Bank of England. Young Fauquier's uncle William became a merchant and a director of the South Sea Company. The family connections plus Francis' sound views on taxation published in a popular pamphlet led to his appointment. He substituted for General Jeffrey Amherst, the British military commander in America, who was also nominal Governor of Virginia, but never visited the colony, being too busy elsewhere with other matters. Francis Fauquier possessed many traits which combined to make him a well-loved governor during the very difficult time preceding the American Revolution. He had a scientific mind, was musical, humane, polished, and genuinely interested in Virginia and its people. Some time after the Revolution, Thomas Jefferson described him as "the ablest man who ever filled the chair of government here."

As to the organization of the new county, the list of justices included the name of Thomas Marshall, whose infant son John was later to become Chief Justice of the United States Supreme Court. Henry Churchill became county lieutenant, Joseph Blackwell, sheriff, and Humphrey Brooke, clerk. The first court was held in the house of William Jones on the lands of Richard Henry Lee. Since then, there have been six different courthouse buildings erected in close proximity, in the years 1760, 1762, 1790, 1818, 1853 and 1889. Records have been preserved, although two serious fires occurred in the two most recent structures. The present courthouse is said to have been designed by William H. Baldwin.

Andrew Edwards was permitted a license to keep an ordinary when the first courthouse was established, and the "Red Store" operated by Scottish merchant Alexander Cunningham from Dumfries was opened for business. A classical school was opened in 1777 by a Princeton graduate, Hezekiah Balch, on some of the Lee lands and named "Warren Academy" after the hero of the Battle of Bunker Hill. It was from this establishment that Warrenton took its name, by which the community was known for thirteen years before achieving official status as a municipality in 1810.

In 1835, Joseph Martin's *Gazetteer* . . . had this to say about the thriving little metropolis:

"It is a beautiful village situated near the center of the county; and contains (besides the ordinary county buildings which are spacious and handsome, and erected at an expense estimated at $30,000) 200 neat and closely built dwelling houses, 3 houses of public worship, Methodist, Presbyterian and Episcopalian, 4 primary schools, 3 taverns, 4 private boarding houses, 2 printing offices, each issuing a weekly paper, 4 wheelwrights, 1 coach maker, 3 saddlers, 1 hatter, 2 boot and shoe factories, 2 cabinet makers, 5 house carpenters, 4 blacksmith shops, 2 tailors, 2 clock and watch makers, 3 bakers, 1 tanner and currier, 3 breweries, 1 tin plate worker, 2 milliners, 1 mantuamaker, 1 house and sign painter, and 2 plough manufactories. This village has a regular market, which is held in a neat little building, the upper part of which is used as a Town Hall. Population 1300; of whom 3 are resident ministers, 9 attorneys, and 8 physicians. The Winchester, Fredericksburg, Alexandria & Charlottesville, post roads intersect each other at right angles in Warrenton, which makes it quite a thoroughfare. Many travellers going south prefer this route as it gives them an opportunity of viewing the rich counties at the foot of the Blue Ridge . . . and of visiting the University of Virginia. There is an excellent McAdamised turnpike from Warrenton to Alexandria.

County Courts are held on the 4th Monday in every month; Quarterly in March, May, August and November."

The first settlement in what is now Fauquier County was probably "Germantown" on Licking Run about eight miles south of Warrenton. The first inhabitants came from Westphalia in Germany and were ironworkers, brought to Virginia by Governor Spotswood with the assistance of the Swiss Baron de Graffenreid to operate his iron furnaces in Essex County (later Orange Co.) where they had settled in 1714 in a village called Germanna. They moved to the new town about 1720, where they were granted 1,800 acres of land in 1724 by Lord Fairfax.

Several other towns developed or were planned along the Rappahanock including Carolandville on the lands of Landon Carter, but they no longer exist.

Rectortown, incorporated as Maidstone in 1772 was first named after Lord Fairfax' estate in England, but common usage had it named after the trustee, John Rector, on whose land it was established. Marshall was incorporated in 1796 as Salem, changed in 1882 to the present name, probably honoring Chief Justice John Marshall. Opal was incorporated as Fayettesville in 1798, and was later known as New Brighton. Paris, probably named to honor Lafayette, was authorized in 1819, as was Upperville, which was formerly known as Carr Town. New Baltimore, formerly Ball's Store, was officially sanctioned in 1822. In the names of some villages, natural features are noted, such as The Plains, which was formerly called White Plains after the outcroppings of white quartz prevalent in the area, and Sumerduck which was named after the large flocks of wild fowl which used to migrate there each year.

Even before Fauquier County became separated from Prince William, it was laced with main roads from north to south, east to west, traversing uninhabited lands for long distances. Ordinaries were of importance to the many travelers as well as to the small number of local residents in the early times who depended on the highly respected keepers for news of all kinds and for official notices. The following is quoted from "Fauquier County, Virginia, 1759-1959":

"Five of these ordinaries were located on the map of the early thoroughfares in Fauquier: Covington's, on the old Marsh road; Hardin's, at the junction of the German Path with the Shenandoah Hunting Path; Neavil's, considered the most important, located at the crossroads of the Carolina and Dumfries Roads; Jos. Neavil's, on the Dumfries (Falmouth) Road to the Valley; Watts', at the corner where the Dumfries Road to the Valley crossed the Manassas Gap Road; Lawrence's, on Dumfries Road, beyond Jos. Neavil's."

Agriculture and stock raising have always been the main industries since the first English settlement in Fauquier. Oxen were the main beasts of burden during the 1700's and 1800's. Brick kilns, tanneries, distilleries, woolen and grist mills also furnished products which were in demand at home and abroad.

When in 1775 the Burgesses met in Williamsburg and formed a Revolutionary Convention, they divided the colony into eighteen districts, one of which was made up of Orange, Culpeper and Fauquier Counties. The regiment of three hundred and fifty men was organized and was called the "Culpeper Minute Men". The three top officers were Colonel Lawrence Taliaferro, Lieutenant Colonel Edward Stevens and Major Thomas Marshall. John Randolph described them in the United States Senate thus: "They were raised in a minute, armed in a minute, marched in a minute, fought in a minute and vanished in a minute." Their flag depicted a coiled rattlesnake with the words, "Don't tread on me," and they wore green hunting shirts on which were the words, "Liberty or Death" in large white letters. Bucktails were stuck in their hats and they carried tomahawks and scalping knives in their belts. The one hundred and fifty who were armed with rifles took part in the first battle of the Revolution to be fought in Virginia, at Great Bridge in December, 1775.

Lord Fairfax had subdivided his Northern Neck Proprietary and created the "Manor of Leeds", named after Leeds Castle, a family seat in Kent, England. The Manor contained 122,850 acres and was bounded by Hedgeman River, Carter's Run, Goose Creek and the Blue Ridge Mountains between Happy Creek Gap and Ashby's Bent Gap. It was this territory, lying in what are now Fauquier and Loudoun counties, which young George Washington helped survey.

Washington wrote the following description of "My Journey Over the Mountains, in 1748". He was with a surveying party which followed the trail through what is now Fauquier: ". . . we got our Supper and was lighted into a Room and I not being so good a Woodsman as ye rest of my Company stripped myself very orderly and went in to ye Bed as they called it when to my Surprise I found it to be nothing but a Little Straw-Matted together without Sheets or anything else but only one thread Bear blanket with double its Weight of Vermin such as Lice Fleas &c I was glad to get up (as soon as ye Light was carried from us) I put on my Clothes and Lay as my Companions. Had we not been very tired I am sure we could not have slep'd much that night I made a Promise not to sleep so from that time forward chusing rather to sleep in ye open Air before a fire as will appear hereafter."

At Frederick Town (now Winchester) the following day he noted, "we cleand ourselves to get rid of ye Game we had catched ye Night before."

When Lord Fairfax died in 1781, his will named his nephew, the Reverend Denny Martin, as beneficiary provided he would take the Fairfax name and coat of arms. The Commonwealth of Virginia asserted a claim to the estate on the grounds that the Reverend Denny Martin Fairfax was a British subject inimical to the liberties of Americans. While that case was in litigation, the Court of Appeals in Virginia, and the Supreme Court of the United States proposed that the heirs relinquish claims to all lands which were waste and unappropriated at the time of Lord Fairfax' death. The Courts directed that the heirs be given possession only of those lands which Lord Fairfax had claimed for his personal use by deed or survey. John Marshall, later Chief Justice of the United States Supreme Court negotiated with the Reverend Mr. Fairfax, and after his death, with his brother, Philip Martin, for purchase of the Manor of Leeds. In 1808 John Marshall and his brother James acquired this and two other tracts totalling about 40,000 acres. The greater portion was divided by the brothers and the remainder was partitioned by commissioners appointed by the Fauquier Court in 1845.

Presley Neville O'Bannon, who was born in Fauquier County, was appointed a second lieutenant in the United States Marine Corps in 1801. While battling against the Barbary pirates in protection of his country's commerce, he led a force of recruits to the Fortress of Derne where American seamen were imprisoned on the "Shores of Tripoli". The successful outcome of the engagement resulted in the first planting of the United States flag on foreign soil.

On the occasion of General Lafayette's return visit to the United States, a large deputation met the General and his Culpeper County escort at the county line on the north bank of the Rappahannock in September, 1825. They escorted him to Warrenton where a gala dinner was given after an enthusiastic reception by the people of the town and a company of boys appropriately uniformed for the occasion as the Lafayette Guard.

A Warrenton attorney, John Quincy Marr was the first Southern officer killed during the Civil War. He lost his life at Fairfax Courthouse in June, 1861. John Singleton Mosby organized his Rangers in 1863 and they saw extensive and unusual service to the cause, operating for the most part in the area referred to as Mosby's Confederacy including territory in both Loudoun and Fauquier Counties.

After the Civil War, many Northerners came to Fauquier and bought up large estates on which they continued some of the traditions of fox hunting and the breeding of fine cattle and horses. Among the outstanding sporting and social events are the annual Gold Cup Races held in the Warrenton area.

The Fauquier Historical Foundation was organized in 1965 to preserve historical landmarks, their first project having been the restoration of the old jail and conversion of it into an historical museum. The old Auburn Mill, close to the site of Neavil's Ordinary, has been restored by the Warrenton Antiquarian Society.

It also owns and maintains Weston, the home of Giles Fitzhugh who "seated on Cedar Run in 1753" on land which he secured from Charles Carter, to whom it had been granted by his grandfather, Robert Carter, in 1725.

WEST VIEW . . . Richard deButts built this home about 1830 upon a plan reminiscent of plantation homes of the deep South with a high English basement. An interesting tale is that he wagered and lost West View in a poker game on a Mississippi River boat. The present owners are the fourth generation to make it their home. Route 623, near Upperville.

ASHLAND FARM . . . The Holtz-claw family acquired the original grant in 1725 and the estate, called "Ashlawn" on the old maps, remained in the family for over a century. It was sold in 1928 to the present owners who had architect Laurence Bottomley remodel it into a hunting lodge. Route 681 near Warrenton.

BOXWOOD . . . Built 1826 by William Swart, with extensive additions in 1925. It is the former home of General "Billy" Mitchell, early advocate of air power. Near Middleburg.

— 158 —

GLEN ORA . . . Given a name of Scottish origin, this house was built in 1810, with farm buildings which may be a decade or two older. In 1960, the late President John F. Kennedy leased the estate as a family retreat. Near Middleburg at Routes 776 and 627.

## MIDDLEBURG - UPPERVILLE AREA

HERONWOOD . . . House, resembling a small chateau, has an inner core of a farm house built in the 1700's. The garden has a notable collection of topiary in box and yew, including nine-foot boxwood peacocks, perhaps the finest topiary pieces in America. Near Upperville, south of Route 50 on Route 623.

OLD CORNER . . . Erected in the early 1800's, it is structurally unchanged. The living room was originally a country store. The small stone building in the yard was a Doctor's Office in 1804; now loaned to the village of Upperville as a library. In Upperville.

MONTMORENCY . . .
The rear portion of this house is probably much older, but the front portion was added in 1840 by John Kerfoot who had purchased this part of the Landon Carter patent in 1822. 3 miles south of Upperville on Route 712.

BROOKMEADE FARMS . . . Part of a grant in 1724 to John Warner, an early surveyor; later the home of William Fairfax. Situated at the foot of the Blue Ridge Mountains, it is famous for thoroughbred horses. Cavalcade (Kentucky Derby winner) is buried here. It is the home of Sword Dancer, 1959 "Horse of the Year". Near Upperville.

THE PONDEROSA . . . Against a backdrop of mountains, this delightful inn is owned and operated by the Cartwrights, who specialize in serving fine food in a fashion and setting that would please the most discriminating taste. It was originally the home of Channing Delaplane. Near Paris on Route 17.

PARIS
AREA

OVOKA . . . The original house of four rooms was built about 1731 on part of the George Carter patent and was the home of Charles Stevins who maintained the first trotting racetrack in Northern Virginia. George Washington is said to have spent several nights here in 1748 while surveying the trail west through Ashby's Gap on his way to Lord Fairfax's "Greenway Court". The main part of the house was built in 1830. The estate's more than a thousand acres include some of the oldest houses still standing in the village of Paris. It has remained in the same family for many generations. Near Paris.

YEW HILL . . . A typical early pioneer home, it should stand sturdily for two more centuries as a landmark of a wilderness outpost of civilization in the highlands of Fauquier. It was erected about 1760 by Robert Ashby on a grant secured in 1742 by his father, Thomas Ashby. George Washington made this home his headquarters from March 9th to March 18th, 1769 while on a survey trip. While there, he was visited by Colonel Thomas Marshall, the father of John Marshall. Route 17 near Delaplane.

LEEDS EPISCOPAL CHURCH . . . The Parish of Leeds was formed from part of the Parish of Hamilton in 1769. The present building was erected in 1842, repaired after a fire in 1873, and given extensive additional repairs in 1930. Near Markham.

## MARKHAM AREA

GIBRALTAR . . . A pioneer house with thirty inch brick walls, built in 1750. A stone wing was added in 1790 by Dr. George Brooke whose wife was a sister of Chief Justice John Marshall. It was restored in 1950 and a kitchen wing added. A mile south of Markham.

ASHLEIGH . . . Built about 1845 by a grand-daughter of Chief Justice John Marshall, Margaret, and her husband (a cousin) John Thomas Smith, on her portion of the Oak Hill estate. An old servant who lived there during the Civil War said that "Miss Margaret" returned from a visit to the South with the "pattern" of the house, similar to "Greenleaves" in Natchez. Route 17 near Delaplane.

DELAPLANE AREA

OAK HILL . . . In 1773, Colonel Thomas Marshall moved from his old log dwelling on Goose Creek called "The House in the Hollow" and bought 1,700 acres east of Cobbler Mountain and built the first house at Oak Hill, which he called "The Oaks". It was a seven room frame building with dormer windows similar to Williamsburg cottages. The present Oak Hill was built by Chief Justice John Marshall for his son, Thomas Marshall in 1818. Route 55 near Delaplane.

WAVERLY . . . Built in the early 1900's, on an estate which specializes in show horses. These horses receive their summer training here and are taken to Florida for the winter. They are active in the Warrenton Hunt and receive many prizes at the annual Warrenton Horse Show which is held each Labor Day Weekend. Located on Route 802 near Warrenton.

SHIRLAND HALL . . . Built by William H. Fletcher about the time of his marriage to Harriet Lake in 1827.

RECTORTOWN
AREA

WOOLF'S MILL . . . In 1798 Vincent Moss sold to Caleb Whitacre "a lot of land on which the said Whitacre has built a mill and now lives". The mill was later owned by the Mc-Clanahans, whose daughter married Frank Woolf, in whose family it remained for many years, hence the name. It is beautifully preserved. Route 624 near Rectortown.

SUDLEY . . . This house was erected in 1839 by Richard H. Carter, additions were made by Mrs. Henly Carter in 1932 and by the present owner in 1960 and 1965. The garden was designed by Rose Greeley in 1943. Near Marshall.

## BETWEEN MARSHALL AND THE PLAINS

DONDORIC . . . The plantation, first called "Mountain View" was owned by the Horner family for more than a century. The house was built in 1818 by Richard Brent Horner on the site of his mother's home which had been burned.

BELVOIR HOUSE . . . Erected in 1792 by Richard Rixey on the site of the home of Bryan O'Bannon, it was restored in 1906 by the Fairfax Harrisons. This 1,000 acre estate is now an important horse-breeding and training farm with both outdoor and indoor tracks. Near The Plains.

## THE PLAINS

GORDONSDALE . . . Erected in 1818. The 2,023 acre estate was granted in 1726 to Parson Alexander Scott. It remained in the Scott and Peyton families until 1878. Aside from the handsome mansion, there is a fine log cabin built in 1776 by John Scott, nephew of the Parson. Near The Plains.

GRACE EPISCOPAL CHURCH
. . . Consecrated June 28, 1918, it replaced the original edifice which had been consecrated July 1, 1855 by Bishop William Meade. The bell from the old church is in the fine building. It was erected from stone contributed from nearby farms including a gift by A. C. Furcron of stones from the ruins of the original Glebe House which had been built about 1772 on his farm near The Plains.

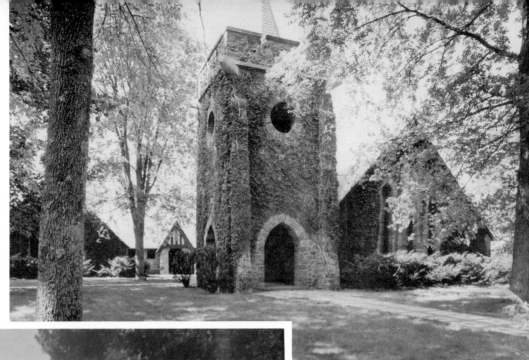

ROCK HILL . . . Also called "Greystone", was constructed of quarried stones of two sizes which were laid in courses similar to Flemish Bond brickwork, with the date of October 7, 1807 cut into one stone. It was built by Minor Winn Junior, a Trustee of the town of Salem which was established in 1796 and later renamed Marshall in 1882. Minor Winn had inherited the 228 acre property from his father who had leased it in 1764 from Colonel Richard Henry Lee and erected thereon a small stone house in 1775. Route 626 near The Plains.

KINLOCH . . . Built in 1823 by Thomas Turner IV who married Elizabeth Carter Randolph, the home was partially destroyed by fire in 1831 and rebuilt two years later. Much of Robert E. Lee's boyhood was spent here visiting his relatives. His horse, Traveler, which he rode throughout the Civil War was named for a beloved mount of his boyhood days at Kinloch; "Fancy Traveller". When Augustine Washington of Waveland Plantation, near Marshall, volunteered in the Confederate Army, he sent the Mount Vernon silver by ox-cart, covered with fodder, to his friend Edward Turner for safekeeping at Kinloch. Near The Plains.

LORETTA . . . Originally called "Edmonium", the oldest portion was built about 1741 by Elias Edmonds. It was added to by his son's widow about 1800 with money received for the Revolutionary services of Major Elias Edmonds Jr. It passed into the Foote family through the widow's marriage to Richard H. Foote, who, according to legend, buried his silver in the yard during the War of 1812 and died without revealing its location. The house was built on an old Indian burying ground, and has many fascinating ghost stories, related in "Virginia Ghosts" by Marguerite duPont Lee. Renamed "Loretta" by a schoolgirl for a nun she admired. Bethel Road near Warrenton.

## NORTHWEST OF WARRENTON (ROUTE 17)

HOPEFIELD . . . Built in 1814, with additions in 1924. Near The Plains.

OLD JAIL . . . When it appeared that the jail, with the jailer's house, erected in 1778, might be destroyed when replaced by a new jail on a different site in 1965, a group of representatives of civic and historical associations organized the Fauquier Historical Foundation to acquire the buildings and operate them as a museum. These are the oldest public buildings in Warrenton. Nearby is the Warren Green Hotel, erected in 1819, destroyed by fire about 1875, and rebuilt the following year, probably using the same walls. Among the famous guests have been General Lafayette, James Monroe, Andrew Jackson, and Henry Clay. Both buildings on Court House Square.

CIVIL WAR SKETCH OF WARRENTON . . .

COURT HOUSE SQUARE, DURING THE CIVIL WAR . . .

MARR HOUSE . . . Built in 1830 by John Marr, father of Captain John Quincy Marr of the Warrenton Rifles. He was the first officer killed in the Civil War, in a skirmish at Fairfax Court House, where a monument stands in his honor. 342 Culpeper St., Warrenton.

MOSBY'S WARRENTON RESIDENCE . . . Built about 1854 by Judge E. M. Spilman, it was purchased in 1875 by Colonel John S. Mosby. The old kitchen and smoke house are in the rear garden. 173 Main St.

WARRENTON

THE KEITH HOUSE . . . Built in 1816 by Thomas L. Moore, opposite the Marr House, the home of his wife's sister; the wives were daughters of Dr. Gustavus Horner. The original early brick courthouse was erected just back of this home in 1762. 127 Culpeper Street.

OAKWOOD . . . The original stone house and 1,500 acres acquired by Colonel Martin Pickett for his Revolutionary War service were given as a dowery to his daughter upon her marriage to Judge John Scott. The Scotts built an addition in 1805 and laid out a beautiful terraced boxwood garden. Their son Robert Eden Scott, who became a distinguished lawyer, was born here in 1808. He was recommended to serve in Lincoln's cabinet. Though opposing secession he remained loyal to Virginia. He was killed in 1862 when making a gallant attempt to capture a party of marauders. Near Warrenton.

## WEST OF WARRENTON

CONWAY GROVE . . . Original portion built in the early 1800's by Dr. James Westwood Wallace of Falmouth, physician to Thomas Jefferson and James Madison. His wife, the former Elizabeth Edmonds of Oak Springs, built another house nearby when they became "uncongenial". 413 Winchester St., Warrenton.

MENLOUGH . . . Originally called "Dixie", it was built in 1853 by Colonel Nathaniel Taylor. Springs Road, near Warrenton.

SOUTHWEST OF
WARRENTON

RIDGLEA . . . Picture is of the coach from Whiffletree Manor before the beautiful Ridglea home; a feature of the Warrenton Gold Cup events held each May. Near Warrenton.

WHIFFLETREE
MANOR

NEPTUNE LODGE . . . Built in 1845 by Governor William (Extra Billy) Smith, and called Monte Rosa. It is said that the fine brick stables were used as a relay stop for mail and stage lines from Washington to Georgia. James K. Maddux purchased it in 1895 and changed the name to Neptune Lodge in honor of his famous race horse. Each upstairs door bears a name plate of a Maddux horse. A local saying is, "there were dinner parties and dinner parties, but none ever to surpass Mr. Maddux's parties at Neptune Lodge." Now it is the scene of the Warrenton Hunt. 521 Culpeper St., Warrenton.

NORTH WALES . . . Part of a 2,900 acre tract patented in 1718 by Captain John Hooe and his brother Rhuys. Original stone house built in 1773, greatly enlarged in 1914 by Walter P. Chrysler Jr. Near Warrenton.

PROSPECT HILL . . . Original house was built in 1811 by Chief Justice John Marshall for his son, Dr. Jacquelin Ambler Marshall. It remained in the family until sold in the 1920's to Lt. Colonel William Doeller, accompanied by the original deed. The house was greatly enlarged, but burned in 1933. Parts of the foundation now form a sunken garden adjacent to the present mansion, built in 1934-35. The Queen Anne architecture was inspired by Bacon's Castle on the James River; the flying stairway is from a Queen Anne house in London; old doors, locks and hinges from the Princess Royal's house in England. Near Orlean.

CABIN BRANCH FARM . . . Built in 1819 and restored in 1934, a delightful and livable house on a working farm of 500 acres. Near Orlean.

FAUQUIER WHITE SULPHUR SPRINGS . . . In the late 1700's Captain Hancock Lee III built a small lodge at these mineral springs on the site of Indian village, and found the waters most efficacious in the easing of the pain of gout. In 1828, his son Hancock Lee IV, in partnership with Thomas Green of Richmond, acquired 3,000 acres and built what was considered the most celebrated and elegant of all Southern spas. In its heyday, "The Springs" entertained 2,000 guests in a season, accommodating as many as 600 at a time, including such notables as Monroe, Madison, Van Buren, Marshall, Clay, Ashby, and Mosby. As one cynical observer described the Spa, "The business of healing and the business of pairing went on furiously side by side, pell-mell, hit or miss—you took the water or you took a mate, or you took both, and with both it was the same—there was no knowing what the effect would be." After the Civil War, the Springs were modestly rebuilt, but burned again in 1901. Since 1957, the Fauquier Springs Country Club has occupied the site. South of Warrenton.

CANTERBURY . . . Magnificent English brick house built in 1932 by J. Temple Gwathmey, selected by French magazine "L'Illustration" as being the most perfect Georgian design. Nearby is "The Cottage", built in 1770 by George Settle who leased the property three years earlier from Lord Fairfax. Around Fauquier Springs, it was known as the Weber Cottage when it was the home of L. F. Weber, noted musician who conducted the concerts at that resort for many years. Near Warrenton.

CHESTNUT LAWN . . . Built in 1832 by Captain James Payne who hired a group of slaves from Mr. Skinker of Goldvein. A stone above the entrance bears the legend "HAN 1832", the initials of Hannibal, the head slave in charge of the work. The stone walls are three feet four inches thick on the first floor, tapering to two feet six inches at the top. Pounds of Minie balls have been found in the yard, and a great oak beam on the top floor bears the impression of a cannon ball. Near Remington.

AUBURN MILL . . . Built in 1769, restored in 1962 by the Warrenton Antiquarian Society, the mill was grinding meal when sixteen year old George Washington accompanied Lord Fairfax through Auburn, staying overnight at Neavil's Ordinary.

MELROSE CASTLE . . . On Rogues Road near Casanova. Architecture inspired by Melrose Castle in Scotland, it was built prior to 1850 by G. W. Holtzclaw of native stone, for the Murray brothers of Scottish ancestry. It was occupied at different times by both armies during the Civil War. Near Casanova.

AIRLIE . . . Occupying 1,200 acres of countryside in the foothills of the Blue Ridge Mountains, this estate belonged to H. C. Groome, a local historian, in the early 1900's. It is now a working conference center where participants come from all over the world to concentrate on different subjects in the beauty and tranquility of this sylvan setting. Route 29-211 north of Warrenton.

# Prince William Heritage

IN 1685, Nicholas Hayward, long a dealer on the Exchange in London with investments in the colonies, conceived the idea of establishing a colony for the Huguenots who were daily coming into England as a result of religious persecution in their native France. He knew that Lord Culpeper had bought out all the other proprietors of the Northern Neck and needed money, so it did not take Hayward long to negotiate the purchase of thirty thousand acres in the County of Stafford. The land was described as being between the Rappahannock and Potomac Rivers, beginning six miles back from the river, between the branches of the Occoquan and extending to the mountains. He formed a syndicate to promote the venture and took in as partners Robert Bristow, who had been involved on the government side in Bacon's Rebellion, Robert Brent and his brother-in-law, Richard Foote.

Hayward began circulating broadsides to the refugees to encourage them to take up lands in the town to be established there and named after the Virginia partner in the venture, George Brent. Each of the colonists was to live in Brent Town on an acre of land and to own a hundred acre farm in the country.

His hopes were not realized because other areas were competing for colonists and those on whom he was depending went instead to Carolina. George Brent then proposed that the land be a refuge and sanctuary for Roman Catholics but this plan did not increase the colonization rapidly either.

The land descended to the heirs of each of the four partners and the boundaries of the tract were so indefinite that it caused a great deal of trouble to Robert "King" Carter when he assumed the Northern Neck Agency and began to issue grants in 1722.

"King" Carter, who had been dismissed in 1711 by Catherine Fairfax as agent for the proprietary, immediately patented grants in the names of sons, grandsons and other descendants until the family owned 90,000 acres in the present counties of Fauquier, Fairfax and Prince William. At one time, the 6,730 acre Lower Bull Run Tract was divided into twelve plantations and references can still be found in the records regarding "Cancer" and "Leo", two of the twelve signs of the zodiac after which they were named. Liberia is the only mansion which still retains its name—derived from "Libra".

A survey of the Brent Town tract was completed in 1738, and the tract was equally divided between the families of the four original partners. Each parcel was dealt with in a different manner, but settlement of them all was now effected. After the Revolution, the Bristow portion was confiscated because the family was ruled "alien" and eventually the title to this quarter was vested in the Literary Fund which divided and sold it in 1834.

When the Treaty of Albany was signed with the Iroquois in 1722, settlement of the Piedmont began in earnest, and the increase in population soon made a new frontier county division desirable. In 1726, a proposal was offered which attempted to divide a new county "Hartford", at Aquia Creek and northward, but the proposal failed. Then in May 1730, two bills were passed, one creating Hamilton parish as of January 1731 and the other creating Prince William County two months later. The latter act included land north of Chopawansick Creek on the Potomac River, but no northern or western boundaries were fixed. It is plain from the wording of the act that not much was known of the Northern Neck geography nor the bounds of the proprietary.

The Governor and Council directed that the Prince William Courthouse be erected on the upper side of Occoquan River at a ferry landing on an estate owned by George Mason III. The building was actually erected on the lower or south side of Occoquan instead. The first clerk was Catesby Cocke, who had been clerk of Stafford. Thomas Harrison was appointed county lieutenant and Robert Jones was appointed sheriff.

The County was named after William Augustus, Duke of Cumberland, the second son of King George II.

Because the rapid settling of the interior continued, further subdividing was desired and on the fifth petition, first Truro Parish, then Fairfax County were formed from the northern portion of Prince William above Occoquan. The courthouse was no longer centrally located for the convenience of the residents of the western portion of the county which went as far as the Blue Ridge Mountains. Five sites were suggested and the Philemon Waters plantation was selected. The site is on the Ashmore farm near the village of Orlando, on Cedar Run. It was here that Henry Lee II acted as presiding justice.

In 1759, Fauquier County was organized and since Dumfries was at this time a very important growing port town, the courthouse was located there by 1761. The early records are lost, and this date is established by a reference in a legal case of the time.

After the decline of Dumfries as a center of commerce, the courthouse was moved to Brentsville on the Brent portion of the Brent Town tract. After the railroad was built through Manassas, it was chosen as the site of the fifth courthouse for Prince William County, and it is still in use.

Prince William County originally contained territory including the present counties of Fairfax, Loudoun, and Arlington plus the City of Alexandria. That area was cut from Prince William with the creation of Fairfax in 1742, and when Fauquier was organized in 1759, another area was taken from Prince William. Each of these changes meant that the courthouse of the time was no longer centrally located in the remaining territory, hence the many changes in the courthouse locations.

A district court was established at Dumfries in 1788 to serve the territory including Fairfax, Fauquier, Loudoun and Prince William Counties. Because the town was not centrally located in the district, a group of commissioners appointed by the Assembly for the purpose selected Haymarket, where a courthouse, clerk's office and jail were built.

Four years later, the cricuit court system was inaugurated which is still in effect, whereby court is held periodically at each county seat. The way in which this old district courthouse became a place of worship is related in the caption of Saint Paul's Episcopal Church on page 182. Bishop William Meade wrote of it in 1857:

"The old courthouse at Hay-Market has been . . . converted into a handsome and convenient temple of religion. A racecourse once adjoined the courthouse, and in preaching there in former days I have, on the Sabbath, seen from the court-house bench, on which I stood, the horses in training for the sport that was at hand. Those times have, I trust, passed away forever."

St. Paul's is the oldest church now existing in Prince William County.

An interesting gravestone, possibly the oldest in Prince William County, was recently moved from Minnieville to Rippon Lodge to preserve it. The inscription, partly on the headstone, partly on the footstone, reads:

"In memory of Rose Peters who departed this life the 10th of September 1690
She is gone, o she is gone to everlasting rest, to
Christ our Blessed Savior who loves sinners best."

Just what her sins were is not known, but there was a Rose Peters who was escorted out of Middlesex in 1685 because of conduct offensive to her neighbors.

The next oldest tombstone in Prince William is that of Martin Scarlet, pictured on page 26. His tombstone and that of his son, John who died in 1697 are on the Deep Hole Farm on Federal property.

Moved to the Pohick churchyard was the tombstone of William Herris which reads as follows:

Heare lyes Bodey of Liut Willeame Herris who died May 16, 1698: Aged 065 Years. By birth A Britaine: A Good Soldier, A Good Husband & Kinde Neighbor."

On July 16, 1861, General Irvin McDowell marched 34,000 inexperienced Union recruits out of Washington on their way to capture Richmond and so to end the war. Their first objective was Manassas Junction, an important rail center where the Manassas Gap Railroad, an east and west line, branched from the Orange and Alexandria, a north and south line. The junction was guarded by 22,000 Confederate soldiers under General Pierre G. T. Beauregard's command. Capture of the junction would insure the Union the easiest route to the Confederate capitol.

General Beauregard urged General Joseph Johnston to bring his 12,000 Confederate troops from Winchester to assist in the defense of the strategic area. Johnston feinted with a mock show of resistance to Union General Robert Patterson and his 18,000 troops at Winchester, then Johnston and his men entrained and rode the Manassas Gap Railroad to the battlefield, arriving the next day.

Two days later McDowell arrived in Centreville. His forces were repulsed by the Confederates at Blackburn's Ford on Bull Run, so he spent two days trying to find a crossing of the run north of the Stone Bridge.

Starting before daybreak on July 21, McDowell's raw recruits stumbled and choked along the rough, dusty lanes to Sudley Springs Ford. They arrived two hours late, but engaged the Confederates in battle and by noon McDowell had the advantage and had almost won, the Confederate lines having broken and retreated. But McDowell paused to regroup his forces and when the battle resumed at two o'clock, the Confederate reinforcements arrived, camouflaged by smoke, dust and the similar colors of uniforms and flags. One unit after another, Union troops fell back until the Confederates rushed their defenses. Retreat turned into rout, and rout into panic and soldiers and sightseers including Senators and Congressmen from Washington who had come out for the day with their picnic lunches, fled back to the Federal City.

Over 40,000 Confederate troops spent the 1861-1862 winter at Centreville in nearby Fairfax County following the First Battle of Manassas, which was also the first major engagement of the Civil War. In March 1862 the Confederates fell back to a new line south of the Rappahannock in anticipation of General George B. McClellan's attack on Richmond.

Three and a half months later Lee pressed McClellan back from the gates of Richmond after several savage battles. Lincoln merged three armies in the Shenandoah Valley and gave General John Pope the command. He started moving his 52,000 troops down the Orange and Alexandria Railroad toward Gordonsville where Lee sent General James Longstreet to reinforce Jackson, making a total Confederate force of 55,000 men.

When captured orders informed Pope of Lee's plan to cut off Pope's retreat to Washington, Pope fell back to the Rappahannock. Then Lee sent Jackson and 24,000 troops around Pope to destroy Federal supplies at Manassas, which Jackson did and then waited for the arrival of General Longstreet and his Confederate reinforcements. After several days of hard fighting, the Second Battle of Manassas ended with the withdrawal of General Pope's forces to the Washington defenses.

BUCKLAND HALL . . .
Thought to have been built under the supervision of the noted architect, William Buckland (designer of Gunston Hall), for Samuel Love, whose grave nearby states that he died in the 60th year of his life in 1787. He was the father of the men who established Kinsley Mill. Temple Mason Washington bought Buckland Hall in 1822, and in 1853 sold it to Major Richard Bland Lee III who had been born at Sully. It remained in the Lee family until recent years. Just east of Lee Highway at Buckland.

BUCKLAND TAVERN . . .
Whereas the town was established by the General Assembly in 1798, it is likely that the tavern had been built much earlier. Lafayette accompanied by a group of dignitaries en route from Warrenton to James Monroe's Oak Hill stopped for refreshments at this tavern where they were feted by a large company of ladies and gentlemen.

FALKLAND . . . The old portion was built about 1800 with later additions. It was the home of John Hill Carter whose original 2,039 acre plantation was once part of Cloverland, his father's estate. Here was born Loughborough Carter, a wild-riding sharp-shooting lad, nicknamed "Nick", who eventually went West and whose exploits in exaggerated form became the basis of the once-popular Nick Carter dime novels. Located two miles off Lee Highway northwest of Buckland.

KINSLEY MILL . . . Three story frame structure on the foundations of an earlier mill which was built about 1794 by John and Charles Love. It is connected by a second story bridge to the old stone granary, with the miller's family quarters in the upper story. Acquired by Daniel Delaplane whose daughter married Orlando Glasscock in 1873, it remained in the Glasscock family. A family cemetery is in the garden of the house, which was rebuilt after a fire in the late 1800's. Half mile east of Lee Highway at Buckland.

SAINT PAUL'S EPISCOPAL CHURCH . . . The building was erected about 1803 to serve as a District Court House, then used as an Academy and by various denominations as a place of worship. It had been purchased in 1822 by William Skinker, Jr., who in 1830 deeded it to the Episcopalians in memory of his wife. It was used as a hospital by the Confederates and later as a stable by the Union Army. Approximately one hundred and twenty-five soldiers from both armies were buried in unmarked graves in the churchyard.

HAYMARKET

THE McCORMICK HOUSE . . . The only house not destroyed by fire when the Federal troops burned the village of Haymarket November 5, 1862. It is across the road from Saint Paul's Church.

BEVERLEY'S MILL . . . This five story stone mill was built by Jonathan Chapman who acquired 650 acres here in 1742. An inscription on a stone high in the wall of the present mill states that the structure was rebuilt in 1858 and establishes the original ownership of Jonathan, who died in 1749, hence we know that the original structure was built before that date. It was badly damaged during the Civil War, being on the route of the Manassas Gap Railroad, and was rebuilt by William Beverley. Nearby are the ruins of the Chapman plantation house, Meadowland. Route 55 at Thoroughfare.

CLOVERLAND . . . Completed before 1797 by Edward Carter (1767-1806), son of Charles Carter of Corotoman and Shirley and half-brother of the mother of Robert E. Lee. The estate was originally within the 12,285 acre Broad Run Tract patented in 1724 by "King" Carter in the names of his sons John and Charles. South of Route 55 near Thoroughfare.

THOROUGHFARE GAP NEAR BEVERLEY'S MILL, where Broad Run flows through a gap in the Bull Run Mountains . . .

LA GRANGE . . . Built by George Green in 1790, then purchased by Benoni Harrison. Though wealthy and a member of the General Assembly, Benoni was small, married to a buxom lass — Catherine Norville, who "ruled the roost." There persists a legend that once, when he crossed her in the presence of visitors, she spanked him soundly. In reciprocation, he built another chimney so that henceforth, they would not share the same hearth. On 681, a half mile from Antioch Church.

THE SHELTER . . . Once a portion of the Bull Run Tract, it was acquired from Samuel Beale in 1789 by Martin Cockburn, who married a cousin of George Mason of Gunston Hall. He was often mentioned in Washington's diary, was a vestryman of Truro Parish, and in 1774 a member of the Fairfax Safety Committee. The estate descended to the Tyler family, and has remained in their possession until quite recently. There is a legend that the dead body of a very old woman, member of a disagreeable family whom the neighbors called the "Rattlesnake Grahams", was carried to the burying ground by relatives because neither horses nor oxen would perform the service. Her unhappy spirit for many years dwelt in a large tree, the stump of which is in the foreground of the picture, upon which even tenacious ivy would not cling. One mile from Woolsey.

EVERGREEN . . . Built in 1827 by Lewis Berkeley, of the James River family, and passed to his son, Captain Edmund Berkeley who served with the Company C, the Evergreen Guard of Prince William. Two and a half miles from Waterfall.

SNOW HILL . . . This was part of the same tract as the Waverley site below, which Lewis Burwell inherited when only fourteen. He later became President of The Council and in 1751 Acting Governor. His son sold 1,064 acres in 1763 to Mathew Whiting, who was living here in 1770 when his own son enrolled at William and Mary. The estate was acquired in 1814 by a relative, Edmund Brooke, grandson of Robert Brooke who was one of Governor Spotswood's Knights of the Golden Horseshoe. Snow Hill is supposedly haunted by the Chief of an Indian tribe, as the house was built on a site sacred to them. Six miles north of Haymarket on Route 15.

WAVERLEY . . . This portion of King Carter's Bull Run Tract was alloted to his grandson Lewis Burwell. It was acquired by Colin Auld of Alexandria in 1836, who conveyed the estate to his nephew, Frederick Foote and offered to back him financially to any extent in the erection of a handsome home. Therefore Frederick built a 17 room house of bricks which were steeped in hot whale oil; but quarrelled with the rich uncle who then refused to pay the bills. Mortgaged to Enoch Pratt of Baltimore, Frederick and his wife managed to carry on through her inheritance, but Pratt bought in their equity upon Foote's death after the Civil War. In 1889, Pratt sold to Eli H. Janney, who enlarged the house by 13 rooms. Janney, a native of Loudoun County, had served in the Confederacy, but was penniless after the war. While clerking in an Alexandria store, he invented the automatic coupling for railroad cars and thereby became wealthy in 1888. In 1902 Waverly was bought by Newland L. DePauw, brother of the founder of DePauw University. Route 15, 2 miles north of Haymarket.

EFFINGHAM . . . Built by Colonel William Alexander who married Sigismunda Mary Massey in 1765. The plantation was inherited in 1814 by his son Lawrence who sold it in 1828 to John Macrae. William Foote purchased it the following year and deeded it to Allen Howison in 1833. One mile southeast of Aden on Route 646.

## NOKESVILLE - BRENTSVILLE AREA

PARK GATE . . . Built about 1750, it was part of the Brent dividend of the Brent Town Proprietary. Thomas Lee purchased the plantation of 795 acres from Daniel Carroll Brent and lived here from 1793 until his death in 1805. He was the eldest son of Richard Henry Lee, signer of the Declaration of Independence. He practiced law and acted in several cases as special attorney for the Commonwealth. His second wife was a niece of George Washington, and is buried here. 1 mile north of Aden on Route 653.

BRENTSVILLE COURT HOUSE . . . Built by William Claytor, this was Prince William County's fourth courthouse, 1822-1892. Restored in 1930 by community funds supplemented by proceeds of a law suit against the builder of a dam on a creek. The dam ruined a swimming hole willed in 1918 by Judge James Bankhead Thornton for public use.

PILGRIM'S REST . . . The earliest documentation involves two deeds, the first from Foote in 1734 to Henry Fitzhugh (1687-1758). A subsequent survey proved that the land acquired by Henry Fitzhugh was not in Foote's portion of the Brentsville Survey, but on land in the name of Hayward from whom Henry Fitzhugh secured a second deed in 1741. He was the son of William Fitzhugh of Chatham. Henry had two sons, John and Thomas, the latter is recorded as living at Pilgrim's Rest. This is possibly the oldest home in Prince William County. Part of the estate lies in Fauquier County, the County line passing between the house and entrance gate. Near Nokesville on Route 600.

MOOR GREEN . . . The land records show 968 acres granted in 1711 to Clement Chevalle and Lewis Reno. Moor Green was willed in 1838 by James Hooe to his sister Jane Foster. It appears in 1860 in the name of James L. Foster, probably her son. One mile north of Brentsville on Route 692.

MANASSAS AREA

LIBERIA . . . Part of King Carter's Lower Bull Run Tract, given to his daughter Priscilla (who married his overseer, Mitchell). They gave 1,660 acres to their daughter, Harriet Bladen Mitchell who married William J. Weir. Their son, Dr. John M. Weir who died in 1852 lies in the family graveyard to the west of the house, with others. General Beauregard made Liberia his headquarters in 1861, and was visited by Confederate President Davis. The following year it was taken by Federal General Sickles for headquarters, and it is said that Lincoln twice visited here.

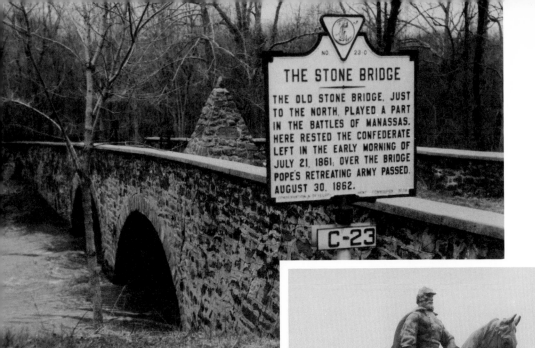

STONE BRIDGE
OVER BULL RUN . . .

MANASSAS NATIONAL
BATTLEFIELD PARK

GENERAL THOMAS JONATHAN JACKSON . . . His firmness during the First Battle of Manassas caused General B. E. Bee to exclaim, "There stands Jackson like a stone wall. Rally behind the Virginians!" Having been through some of the most important battles of the war, he met a tragic death when accidentally shot at dusk by one of his own men in 1863.

OLD STONE HOUSE . . . built about 1812 on the Pittsylvania estate. One end of the house was destroyed by shell fire during the First Battle of Manassas and has a cannon ball still lodged in one wall. Pittsylvania which had been built about 1765 by Landon Carter (1710-1799) was a large frame structure painted the color of dark brick, and was called "the brown house" by wounded soldiers brought there for treatment. It was burned by the Federal troops during the Second Battle of Manassas.

SUDLEY CHURCH . . . The first church on the site was of brick, built about 1800 on land given by Landon Carter and his wife. It was a central point on the "Fairfax Circuit" on which Bishop Francis Asbury rode his white horse. The church was destroyed during the Civil War, where wounded of both armies had been cared for by volunteers. It was rebuilt through the efforts of Colonel Rice of the Federal Army, in appreciation of the kindness of southern people in nursing him after his injuries received in the First Battle of Manassas.

BLACKBURN'S FORD . . . The crossing by Union forces, where Route 28 now crosses Bull Run, brought a lively prelude to the first great combat July 18, 1861.

TRENCHES AND QUAKER GUNS . . . The dummy guns of rough-hewn logs were used to mislead the Federals into thinking the works were heavily fortified. Called "Quaker guns" because of the Quaker belief that killing, even in war, was sinful; these guns were harmless. At Centreville.

CAMP ARCHITECTURE . . . During periods of inactivity, especially in the winter, the men attempted to create a feeling of home by decorating their camps.

DOGAN HOUSE . . . Henry Dogan bought 204 acres in 1787 from Mann Page III (a Carter heir) and erected a large home which was burned shortly before the Civil War. The family then moved into what had been a tenant house, partially built of logs. Now covered with siding, this and the Stone House are the only remaining structures on the Manassas Battlefield.

MANASSAS GAP RAILROAD . . .

— 191 —

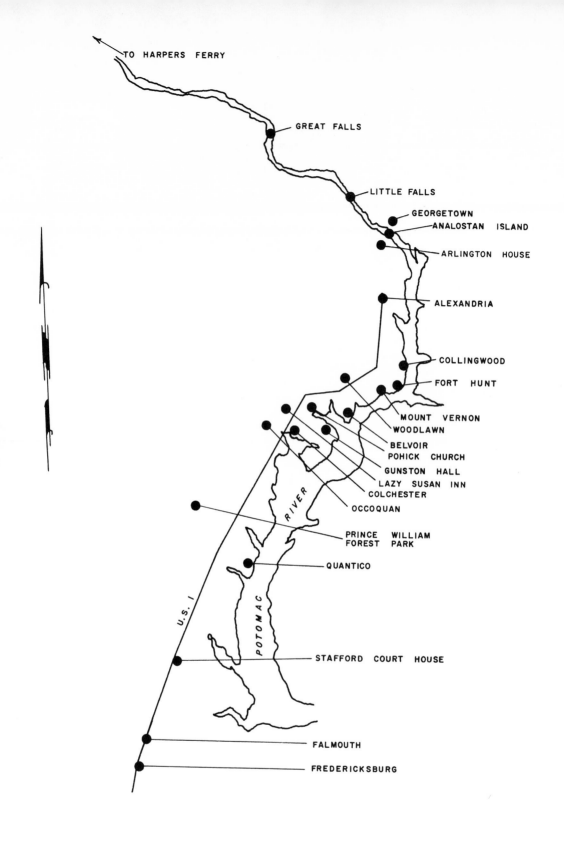

**UP THE POTOMAC**

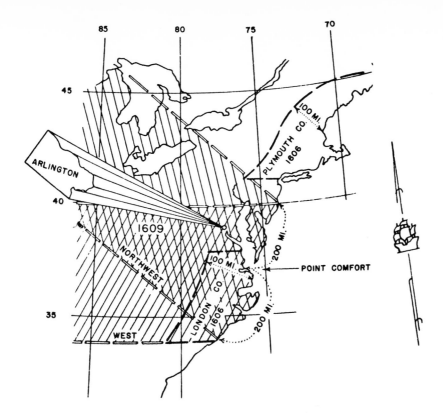

VIRGINIA COLONIES . . . Area included in the early charters of the Virginia Company, which extended to the Pacific.

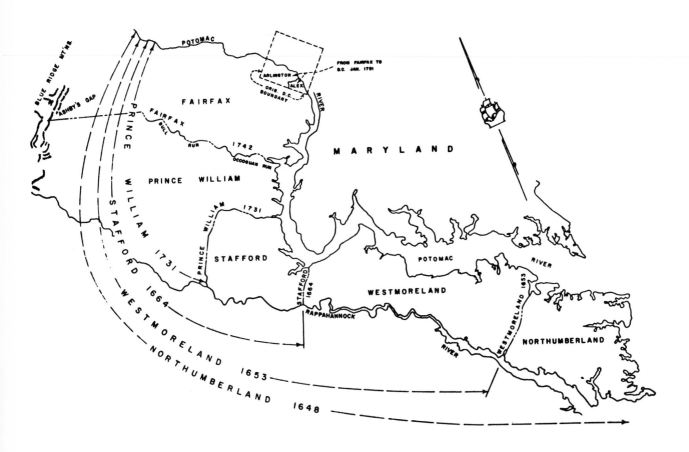

VIRGINIA COUNTIES . . . Sequence of jurisdiction of the area

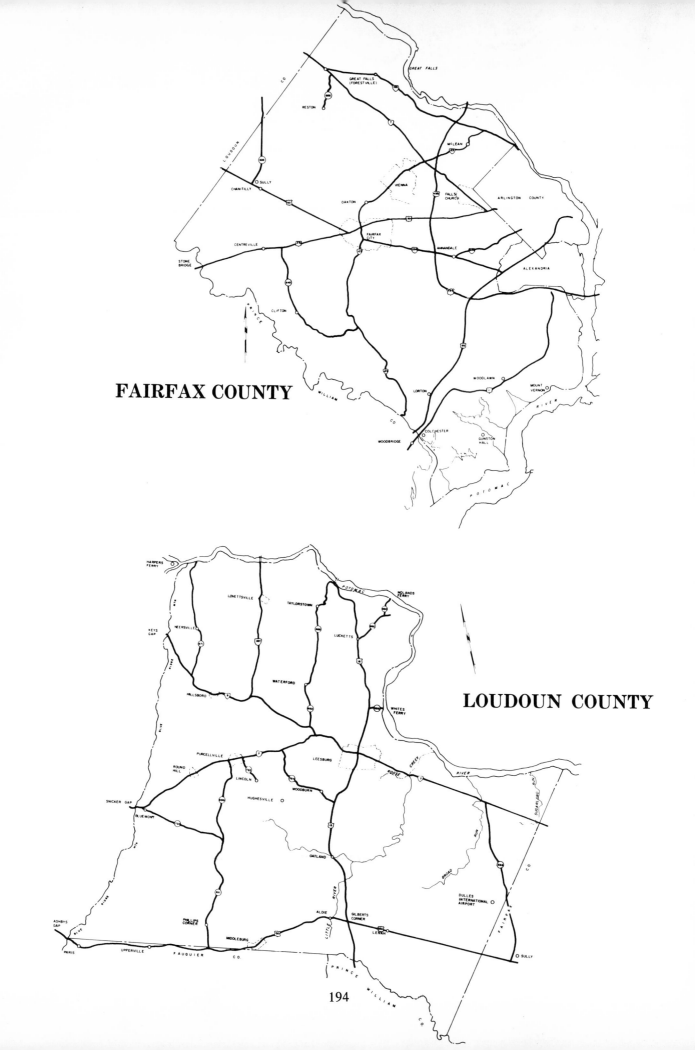

**FAIRFAX COUNTY**

**LOUDOUN COUNTY**

194

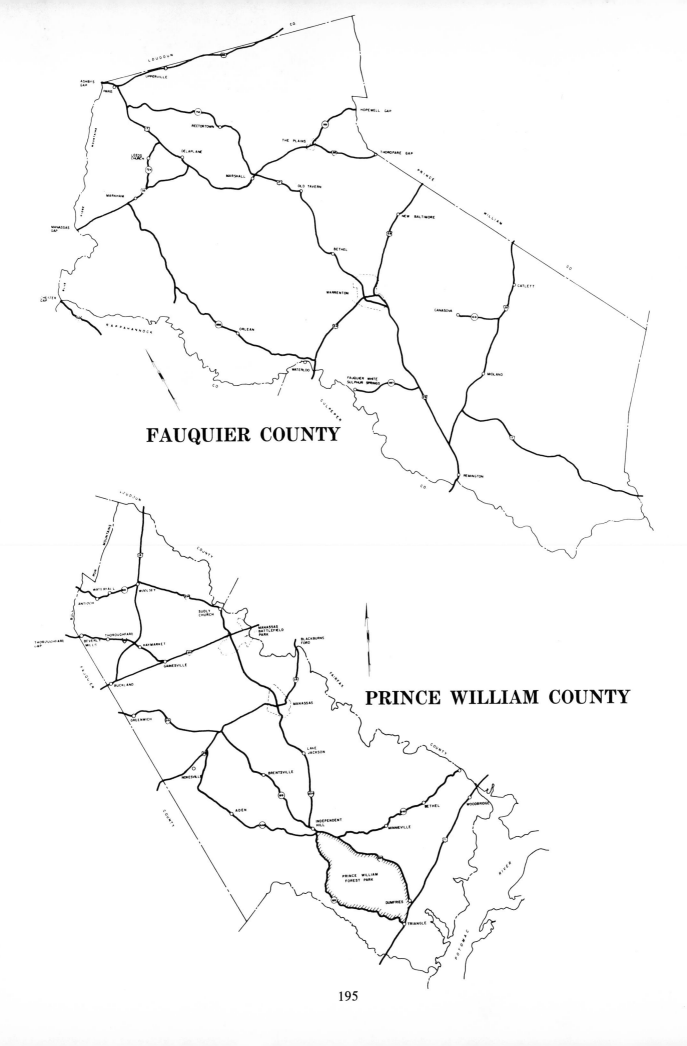

**FAUQUIER COUNTY**

**PRINCE WILLIAM COUNTY**

# Bibliography

Andrews, Matthew Page, "Virginia, The Old Dominion", Doubleday, Doran & Co. Inc., Garden City, 1937.

Arlington Historical Society, "Arlington Historical Magazine", Vol. 2, No. 2, October, 1962.

Bodine, A. Aubrey, "The Face of Virginia", Bodine & Associates. 1963.

Brown, Stuart E., "Virginia Baron", Chesapeake Book Company, Berryville, Virginia. 1965.

Burnaby, Reverend Andrew, "Travels Through the Middle Settlements in North America, in the Years 1759 and 1760 with Observations upon the State of the Colonies." T. Payne, London, 1775.

Caton, James R., "Legislative Chronicles of the City of Alexandria", Newell-Cole Company, Alexandria, Virginia. 1933.

Cooke, John Esten, "Virginia: A History of the People", Houghton Mifflin, Boston. 1897.

Darter, Oscar H., "Colonial Fredericksburg and Neighborhood in Perspective." Twayne Publishers, New York, 1957.

Durham, C.J.S., "Washington's Potowmack Canal Project at Great Falls", The Nature Conservancy, Wildlife Management Institute, and the Fairfax County Park Authority, 1957.

Fairfax County Board of Supervisors, "Industrial and Historical Sketch of Fairfax County Virginia", 1907.

Fairfax County Civil War Centennial Commission, "Fairfax County and the War Between the States", Stenger Typographic Service, Vienna, Virginia, 1961.

Fauquier County Centennial Committee, "Fauquier County 1759-1959", 1959.

Foster, B. G., "A History of Saint John's Church in Fairfax County, Virginia, Parish of Langley", 1917.

Gage, Charles E., "Tobacco, Tobacco Hogsheads and Rolling Roads in Northern Virginia", Falls Church Historical Commission, 1959.

Geddes, Jean, "Falls Church, Virginia: Legends, Lore and Life", Arfax Printing Company, 1962.

Harrison, Fairfax, "Landmarks of Old Prince William", privately published by the author in 1924, reprinted by the Chesapeake Book Company, Berryville, Virginia, 1964.

Head, James W., "History and Comprehensive Description of Loudoun County, Virginia", Park View Press, 1908.

Hebert, Walter H., "Fighting Joe Hooker", Bobbs-Merrill Company, Indianapolis, 1944.

The Historical Society of Fairfax County Yearbooks, Volumes 1-9, 1951-1965.

Hobbs, Horace P., Jr., "Pioneers of the Potowmack", privately published by the author, 1961.

Kabler, Dorothy H., "The Story of Gadsby's Tavern", Newell-Cole Company, Alexandria, 1952.

Lee, Cazenove Gardner, Jr., "Lee Chronicle", New York University Press, 1957, edited by Dorothy Mills Parker.

Lee, Edmund Jennings, M.D., "Lee of Virginia, 1642-1892", Franklin Publishing Company, Philadelphia, 1895.

Lee, Mrs. Marguerite du Pont, "Virginia Ghosts", The William Byrd Press, Inc., 1930. Reprinted by the Chesapeake Book Company, Berryville, Virginia, 1966.

The Library of Congress, Prints and Photographs Division, Historic American Buildings Surveys, 1937 & 1958.

Lindsey, Mary, "Historic Homes and Landmarks of Alexandria, Virginia", Newell-Cole Company, Alexandria, 1931.

Martin, Joseph, "Gazetteer of Virginia and the District of Columbia", Charlottesville, 1835.

McClure, Stanley W., "The Defenses of Washington, 1861-1865", reprinted 1961 by the National Park Service.

Meade, Bishop William, "Old Churches, Ministers and Families of Virginia", Genealogical Publishing Company, Baltimore, 2 volumes, 1966.

Moore, Gay Montague, "Seaport in Old Virginia", Garrett and Massie, Richmond, 1949.

Morton, Richard L., "Colonial Virginia", The University of North Carolina Press, Chapel Hill, 1960. 2 volumes.

Northern Virginia Regional Planning and Economic Development Commission, "Historic Northern Virginia Buildings and Places", 1966.

Reps, John W., "The Making of Urban America: A History of City Planning in the United States", Princeton University Press, 1965.

Rust, Jeanne Johnson, "A History of the Town of Fairfax", privately published by the author, 1960.

Samuels, Harriet Brockman, "Loudoun County, Virginia, Past and Present", The Graphic Arts Press, Princeton, 1940.

Somerville, Mollie, "Alexandria, Virginia: George Washington's Home Town", Newell-Cole Company, Alexandria, 1966.

Sprouse, Edith Moore, "Potomac Sampler", published by the author, 1961.

Steadman, Melvin Lee, "Falls Church: By Fence and Fireside", Falls Church Public Library, 1964.

Stetson, Charles W., "Four Mile Run Land Grants", Mimeoform Press, Washington, D.C. 1935.

Stetson, Charles W., "Washington and His Neighbors", Garrett and Massie, Incorporated, Richmond, 1956.

Strong, Solange, "Old Stone Houses of Loudoun County, Virginia", published by the author, 1950.

Sweet, William Warren, "Virginia Methodism: A History", Whittet & Shepperson, Richmond, 1955.

Swem, E. G., "Virginia Historical Index", The Stone Printing and Manufacturing Company, Roanoke, 1934.

Templeman, Eleanor Lee, "Arlington Heritage", privately published by the author, 1959, 1960, 1961, 1965, 1966.

Templeman, Eleanor Lee, "Northern Virginia Heritage" calendar, Cooper-Trent, Arlington, 1957. Arlington Historical Society.

Tyler's Quarterly: Historical and Genealogical Magazine, Richmond, 1919-1952.

Virginia State Library, "Virginia Cavalcade". Periodical quarterly.

Wayland, John, "Historic Homes of Northern Virginia and the Eastern Panhandle of West Virginia." McClure Company, Inc., Staunton, Va., 1937.

Whitt, Jane Chapman, "Elephants and Quaker Guns", Vantage Press, New York, Washington, Hollywood, 1966.

Williams, Harrison, "Legends of Loudoun", Garrett and Massie, Incorporated, Richmond, 1938.

Williamson, James J. "Mosby's Rangers", Ralph B. Kenyon, 1896.

Wilstach, Paul "Potomac Landings", Doubleday, Page & Company, Garden City, New York, 1921.

Writer's Program, Works Projects Administration, "Prince William: The Story of Its People and Its Places", Bethlehem Good Housekeeping Club, Manassas, Virginia, 1941.

Writer's Program, Works Projects Administration, "Virginia; A Guide to the Old Dominion", Oxford University Press, New York, 1940.

# Acknowledgements

THIS educational and historical book would not have been possible to produce without the wonderful co-operation of many kind persons who assisted us in many ways. Space does not permit a separate mention of each, but you know of your own contribution and of our deep gratitude. We hope that you will share our pride and pleasure in the result.

Aside from the books and materials which we have consulted, the following persons have been most helpful in assisting us in gathering together the fragments of history in their particular areas or have proof-read our material to make suggestions and corrections before the book went to press:

Up the Potomac section of general history of this upper portion of the Northern Neck Land Grant and general history of the area:

Ludwell Lee Montague, a Ph.D. in History, Chairman of the Arlington Cultural Heritage Commission and President of the Society of Lees of Virginia; The Honorable Albert V. Bryan, Judge of the United States Court of Appeals; Jane Nida, Director of Arlington County Libraries; Miss Jeanne Rose, the Virginiana Collection of the same; Dow Nida, former President of the Arlington Historical Society; Miss Josephine Cobb, Specialist in Historical Iconography of National Archives; Pauline Pero, Library of Congress; and Edward Sayle, President of the Arlington Historical Society; John F. Burns and Jack Jones.

For Fairfax County history, we turned to Thomas P. Chapman, Jr., Clerk of the Court and to Corporal Lee Hubbard of the Identification Bureau of the Fairfax County Police Department. Miss M. Patricia Carey, Curator of the Virginiana Collection of the Fairfax County Library and Miss Helen Walker and Mrs. Hannah H. McLay of the Library staff gave great assistance. Mrs. M. C. McFeaters of Falls Church made herself available at all times on short notice for many little chores. Bayard Evans, Chairman of the Historic Landmarks Preservation Commission, C. J. S. Durham, a hard-working member of the Commission, Eddie Printz and Duke Breitenbach with their fine photographs, James Watt of the Fairfax County Park Authority, Joseph Berry of Berry Associates, Mrs. John J. Barnes, III, Alene Anderson, Sheri Dunbar, and Dr. Ross D. Netherton gave us their assistance. Also, John E. Woodall, Information Division; Frank Morse, Librarian at Mount Vernon; Marie D. Smith of Fairfax; and William H. Price of Vienna.

Mrs. Hugh B. Cox, former President of the Historic Alexandria Foundation and the staff of the Alexandria Tourist Council were most helpful, as were Miss Ellen Burke, Director and Miss Margaret Calhoun, of the Virginia Room, Alexandria City Library.

For assistance in the Fredericksburg and Stafford County area, we are indebted to Dr. Oscar H. Darter, historian and author; George H. S. King, genealogist and historian; Mrs. Earle Ware of the Fredericksburg Historical Society; and Colonel Robert Burhans, Curator of Kenmore. Mr. George Gordon, Jr., President of the new Historic Falmouth Towne and Stafford County Historical Society was very helpful.

R. Jackson Ratcliffe of Manassas, Historian of the Prince William County Historical Society furnished a world of information on his part of Virginia, besides lending us many fine negatives of old homes. Mrs. Grace F. Baer of Buckland gave us two fine old etchings of Mount Vernon and Harper's Ferry which you will find reproduced in the "Up the Potomac" section of this book. Mrs. O. Anderson Engh was very helpful.

In Loudoun County, a most generous gift of thirty fine photographs was made to us by Winslow Williams, and the Loudoun County Times-Mirror has loaned us some pictures. We received the enthusiastic moral support of the staff of the Loudoun County Schools, the Loudoun County Chamber of Commerce through the Director, George Hammerly, and James Birchfield, President of the Loudoun County Historical Society. Mr. and Mrs. John G. Lewis of Hamilton were most generous in sharing with us files of historical old houses, and also a wealth of information on the history of the County. Mrs. Robert Pickens of Janelia and Mrs. Stanley Brown of Rockland gave us valuable assistance as did Jean McDonald of Round Hill and Hugh Grubb of Purcellville.

In the Aldie area, Mrs. James Kaylor loaned us the fine photographs which had been taken of historical homes of the area for a benefit tour, Mrs. Harold Potter was very helpful, and Mrs. Ned Douglas loaned us a copy of the beautiful painting of the mill. Colonel Malcolm Kent secured for us the history and pictures of the two manor houses. It was through the gracious cooperation of Mrs. T. U. Dudley of Exning and the good offices of Mr. and Mrs. Walter Hebert of Houston, Texas that we found the charming hunt scene used as the cover of this book. Miss Woodward, Miss Nanny Fred, and Mrs. Mayers at the Colonial Inn furnished some interesting tid-bits of history.

In Fauquier County, we received the assistance of Warren Breth, Director of the Chamber of Commerce; General Lemuel Shepherd, President of the Fauquier County Historical Society; and from Mrs. John Ramey and John Gott, who, although he is Director of Fairfax County School Libraries, is rightfully agreed by everyone to know more about his home county of Fauquier than anyone else. The Fauquier Democrat put their photographic file at our disposal and this is much appreciated. Miss Lucy Duer and Mrs. John Cutting of the Warrenton Garden Club assisted us with pictures.

The excellent maps were made for us by Benjamin Sims, Office Engineer of the Water Division, Arlington County; and Russell Armentrout, Jr. did the artistic lettering for the title.

Among the State officials who were so helpful were John Melville Jennings, Director of the Virginia State Historical Society; Mrs. Katherine Smith of the Virginia Cavalcade and the Virginia State Library; Mr. Irby Hollans, Director of the Virginia State Chamber of Commerce and their official photographer, P. I. Flournoy who gave us many, many fine pictures.

On the National level, we received fine cooperation from the staff of the National Trust for Historical Preservation, with special appreciation to Mrs. Helen Bullock and Robert Garvey, the Director. The staff at the National Archives helped us to find several historic old photographs and prints, as did the members of the staff at the Library of Congress Prints and Photographs Division, Miss Virginia Daiker, Director and two of her assistants, Charles Herrington and Mrs. Renata Shaw. Mrs. Carol Smith, Russell Keune and John Poppeliers of the National Park Service were very helpful; so, too, was Mrs. Elden E. Billings, Librarian of the Columbia Historical Society. Valuable information was furnished to us by Clyde Buckingham, Librarian at the American Red Cross; Thomas McGarry, Special Assistant to the Federal Highway Administrator, United States Bureau of Public Roads; and Margaret Walker, Women's Editor of the "American Motorist," American Automobile Association, Historic American Buildings Survey.

With four hundred and forty pictures, we have made every effort to record the names of each and every photographer. In case any are omitted, we shall try to include them in the next printing if they are properly brought to our attention in writing. We list them alphabetically:

Howard Allen of Allen Studio, Middleburg, Alexandria Gazette, Victor Amato, Robert N. Anderson, Del Ankers, Ollie Atkins, Charles Baptie, The Bemis Company, Incorporated, James Birchfield, A. Aubrey Bodine, Mathew Brady, Duke Breitenbach, John O. Brostrup, John Carter Brown Library, Samuel Chamberlain, Colony Studios of Fredericksburg, Corps of Engineers Museum at Fort Belvoir, Mr. and Mrs. William Curran of the McLean Scene, T. N. Darling, A. J. Del Populo, Mary dePackh, Felix deWeldon, Joy Diehl, Bertha Dougherty, Newbold Noyes and Owen Duval of the Washington Star, Dr. William R. Eastman, Mrs. H. John Elliott of the Garden Club of Fairfax, Embassy of the Netherlands, Fairfax County Chamber of Commerce, the Fauquier Democrat, Federal Aviation Administration, P. I. Flournoy, the Virginia State Chamber of Commerce, the Fredericksburg Information Center; and a father-son team, Paul M. Schmick and Paul A. Schmick of the Evening Star.

Also, John K. Gott, George Mason Green Company, Hugh Grubb of Grubb Photo Lab in Purcellville, Mrs. Stephen Hartwell, George P. Hartzog, Jr., H. H. Harwood, Hastings House, Marshall P. Hawkins, Hessler Studios, Incorporated, of Washington, D.C., Mrs. Omer Hirst, Mrs. Harry E. Howell, Lee Hubbard, Garnet Jex, Russell Jones, Colonel Malcolm Kent, Robert Lautman, John G. Lewis, Library of Congress, Bill Little, Loudoun Times-Mirror, Frank Lyon heirs, Don MacAfee, Henry Mackall, I. Maller, Maryland State Historical Society, Ruth Marler, Mrs. Irving L. Matthews, Robert Pooch McClanahan, Methodist Historical Society, Catherine Moss, Mount Vernon Ladies' Association, Mrs. Charles Morgan of the Fauquier-Loudoun Garden Club, National Archives, National Capital Parks, National Park Service, National Society of Colonial Dames of America, National Trust for Historic Preservation, Nan Netherton, Dr. Ross Netherton, Northern Virginia Conservation Commission, and the Northern Virginia Sun.

In addition, E. H. Olsen, John Ortolani, William M. Peterson, Robert Phillips of Black Star, William W. Phillips, Porter Studio, who gave careful attention to detail on dozens of pictures they processed for us, Eddie Printz, Erle Prior, R. Jackson Ratcliffe, Duncan H. Read, Reston, Incorporated, William M. Rhoden, Riggs National Bank, Jane Robinson, Mrs. Marion Rosengren, Abbie Rowe, Edward B. Russell, librarian of United States Army Engineers at Fort Belvoir, Edward F. Sayle, Mrs. George Slater, Richard B. Smart, Mrs. Carol Smith of the National Park Service, Judson Smith Studios, William Francis Smith, Smithsonian Institution, Robert Strader of the Alexandria Gazette, Bob Templeman, Eleanor Lee Templeman, United States Army History Division, Virginia Cavalcade, Virginia Record, Virginia State Chamber of Commerce, Virginia State Library, Edward Wagstaff, Werneke Associates, Winslow Williams, Mrs. Medora Wolfe of the Alexandria Gazette, John Woodall, Charles Wortham and George Worthington, III.

We have made every effort to furnish accurate information. Many sources have been in contradiction with each other, in which cases we have done much original research in order to divide fact from fiction. However, if any errors are found, we shall be most grateful if corrections are sent to us in writing, giving the documentation or authority upon which the correction is based.

Typography by Imperial Type of Arlington

Binding by Moore and Company of Baltimore

Lithography by Double-Dot of Washington

# INDEX